AFRICA
Coloring Book

Adult Coloring Books

Aryla Publishing 2018

978-1-912675-24-1

www.arylapublishing.com

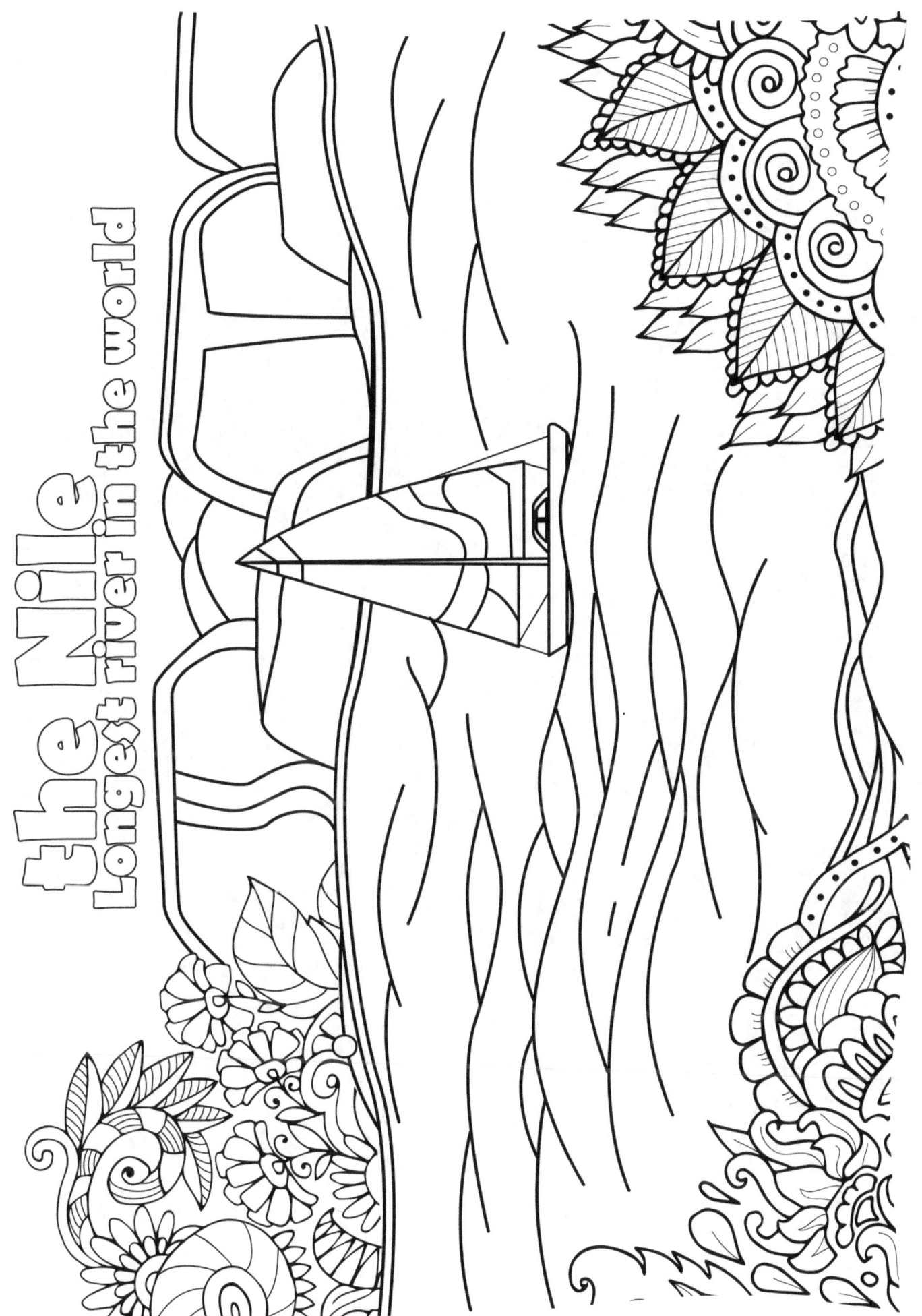

the Nile
Longest river in the world

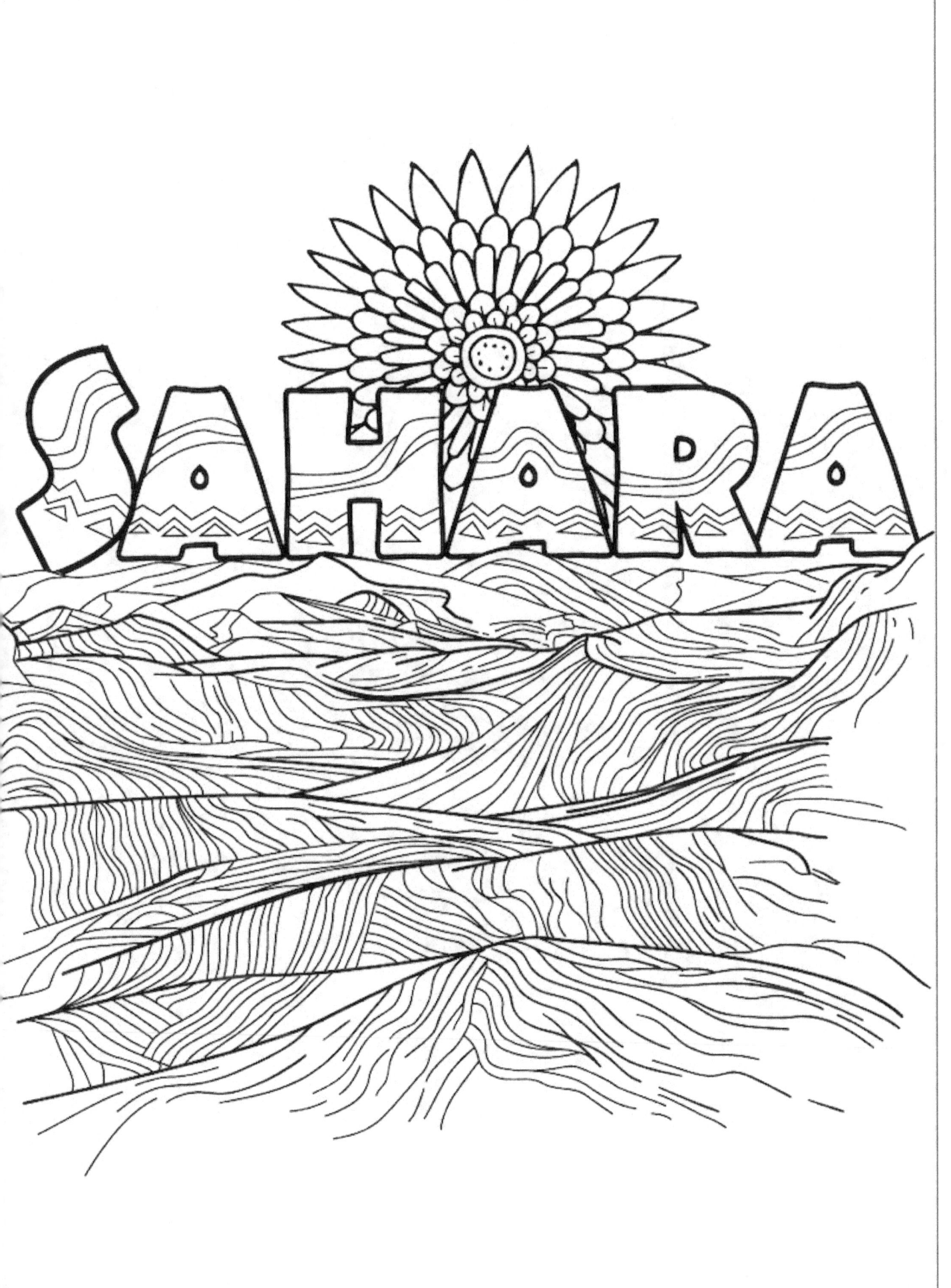

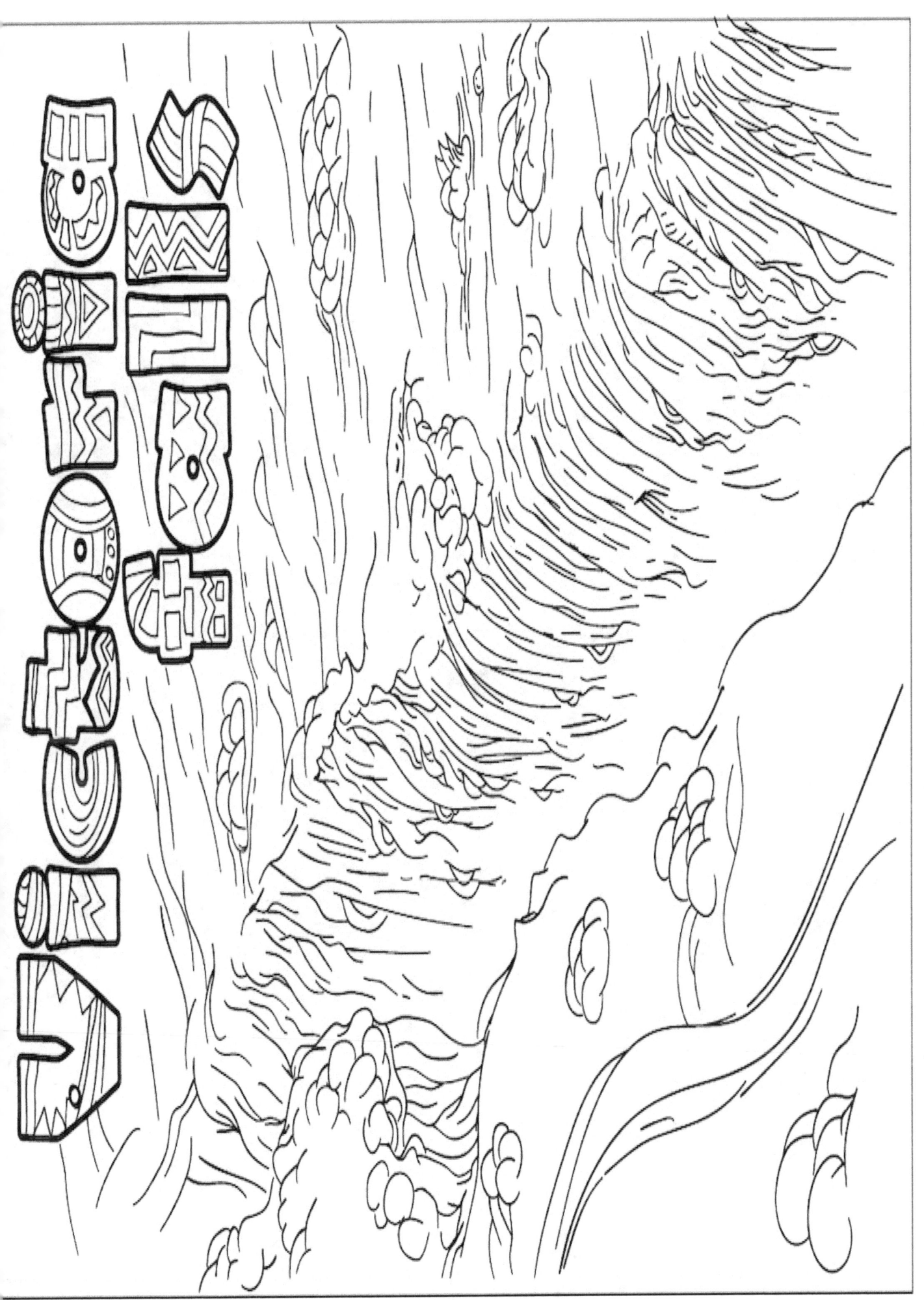

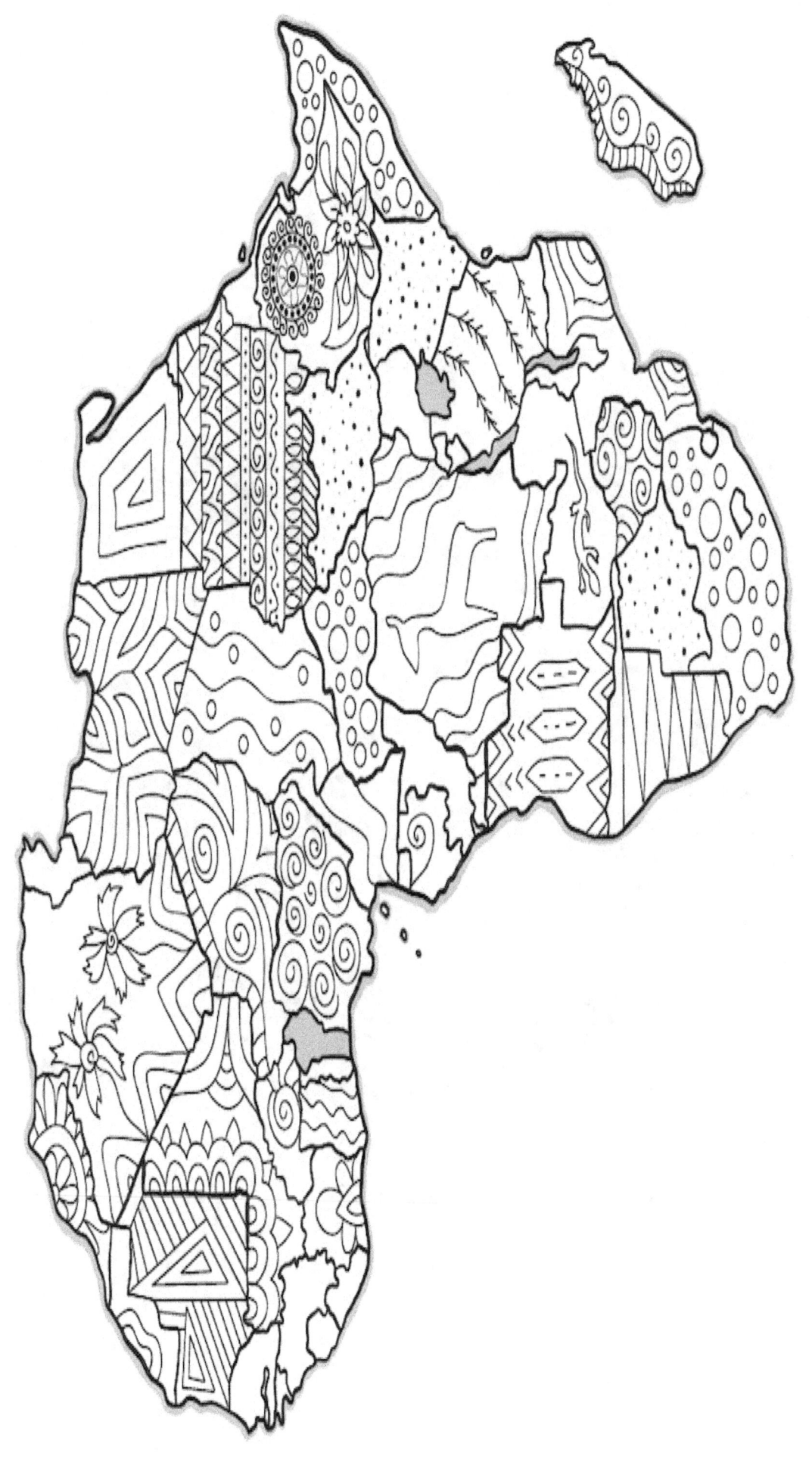

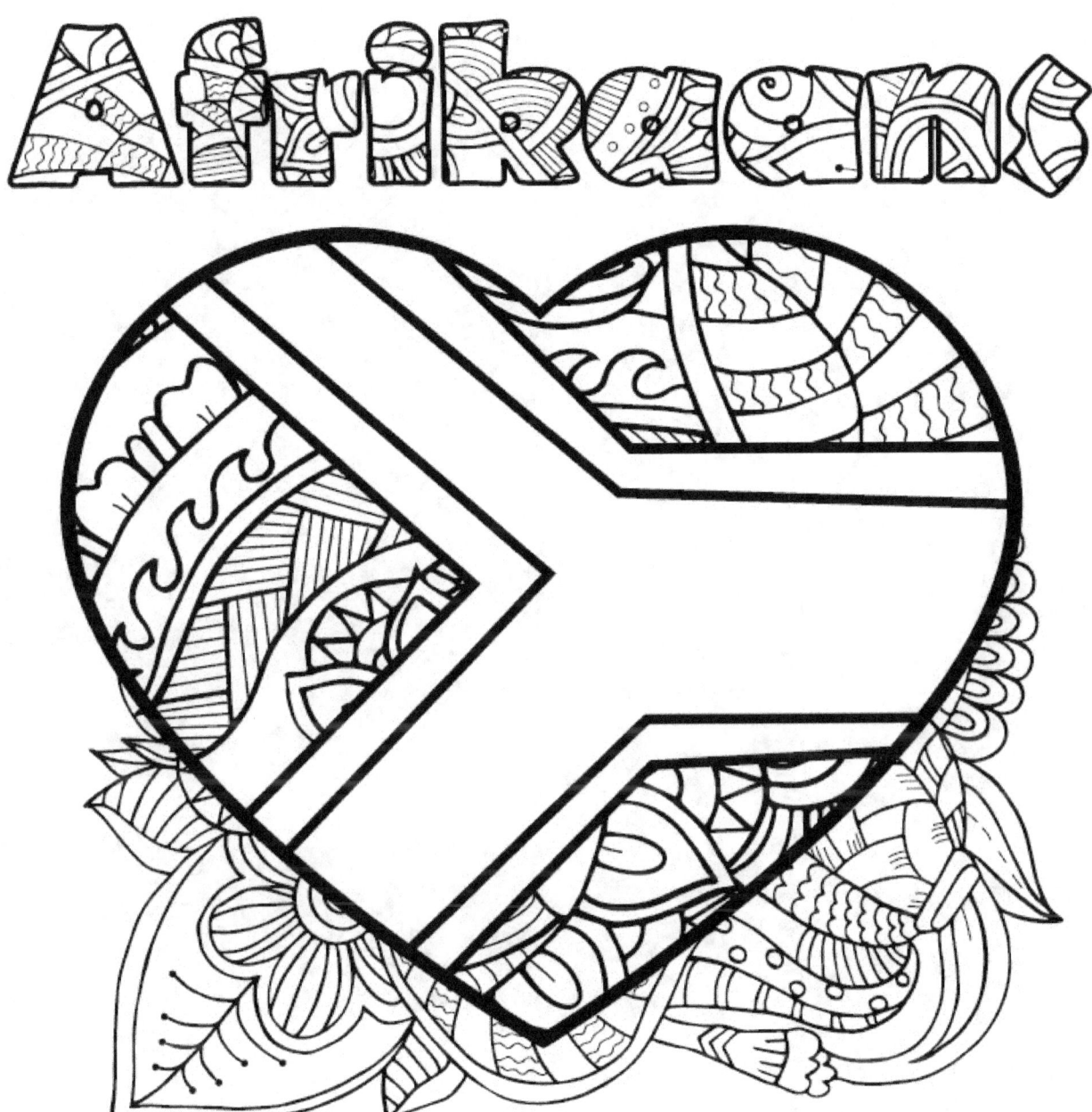

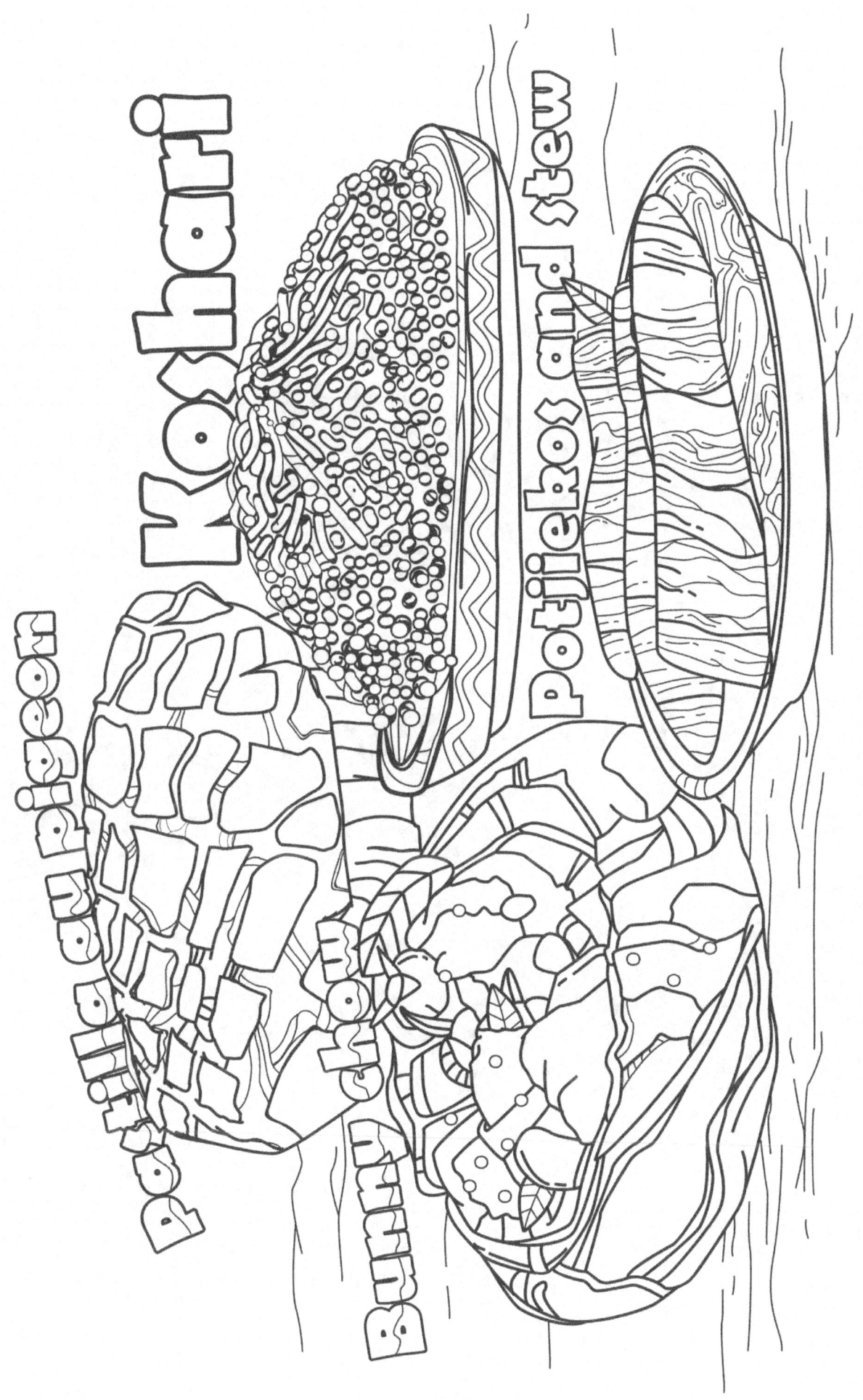

Koshari

Potjiekos and stew

pigeon

Potjiekos pie

Bunny chow

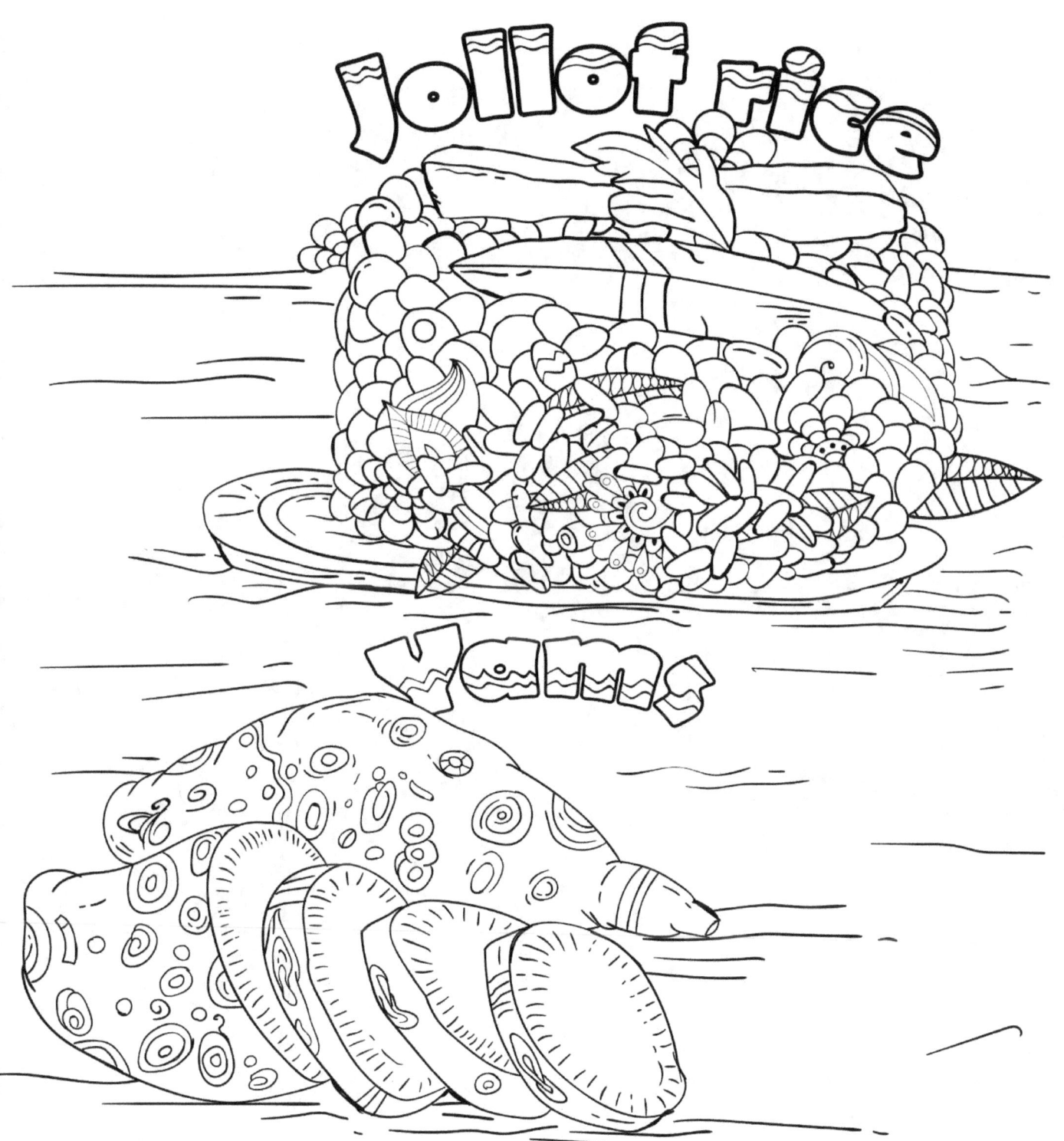

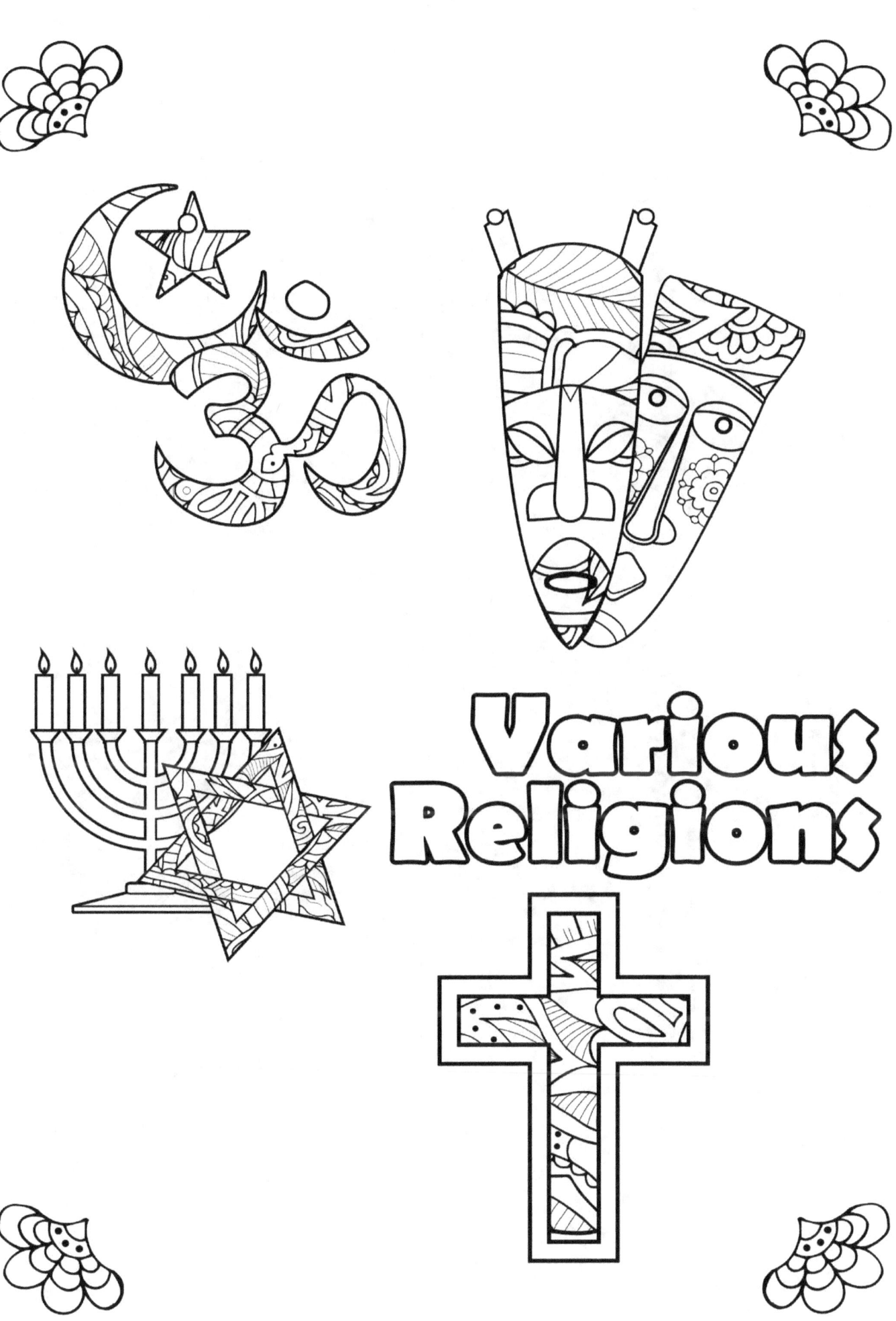

Various Religions

Bartolomeu Dias

the first European who sailed to the southern tip of Africa

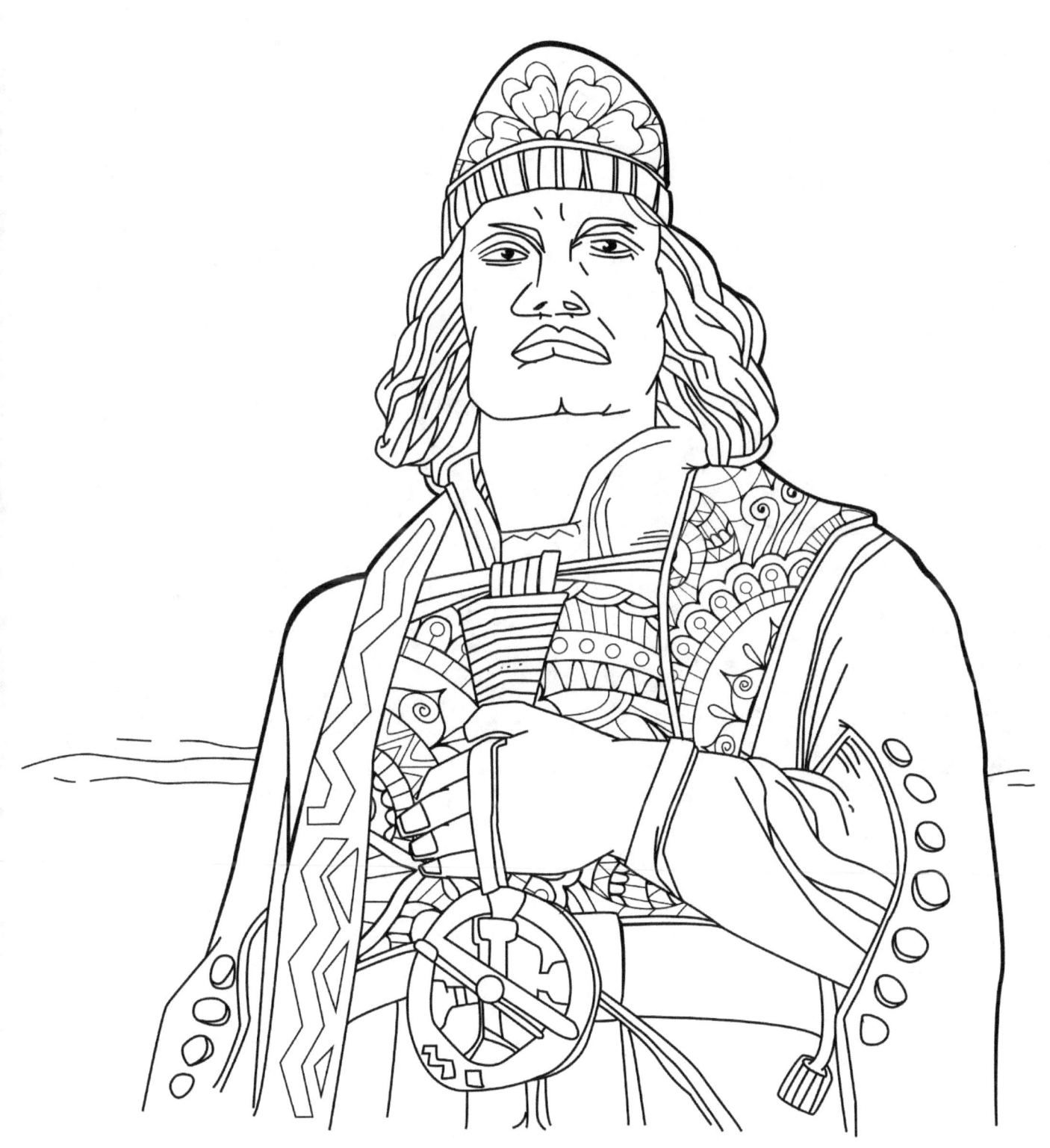

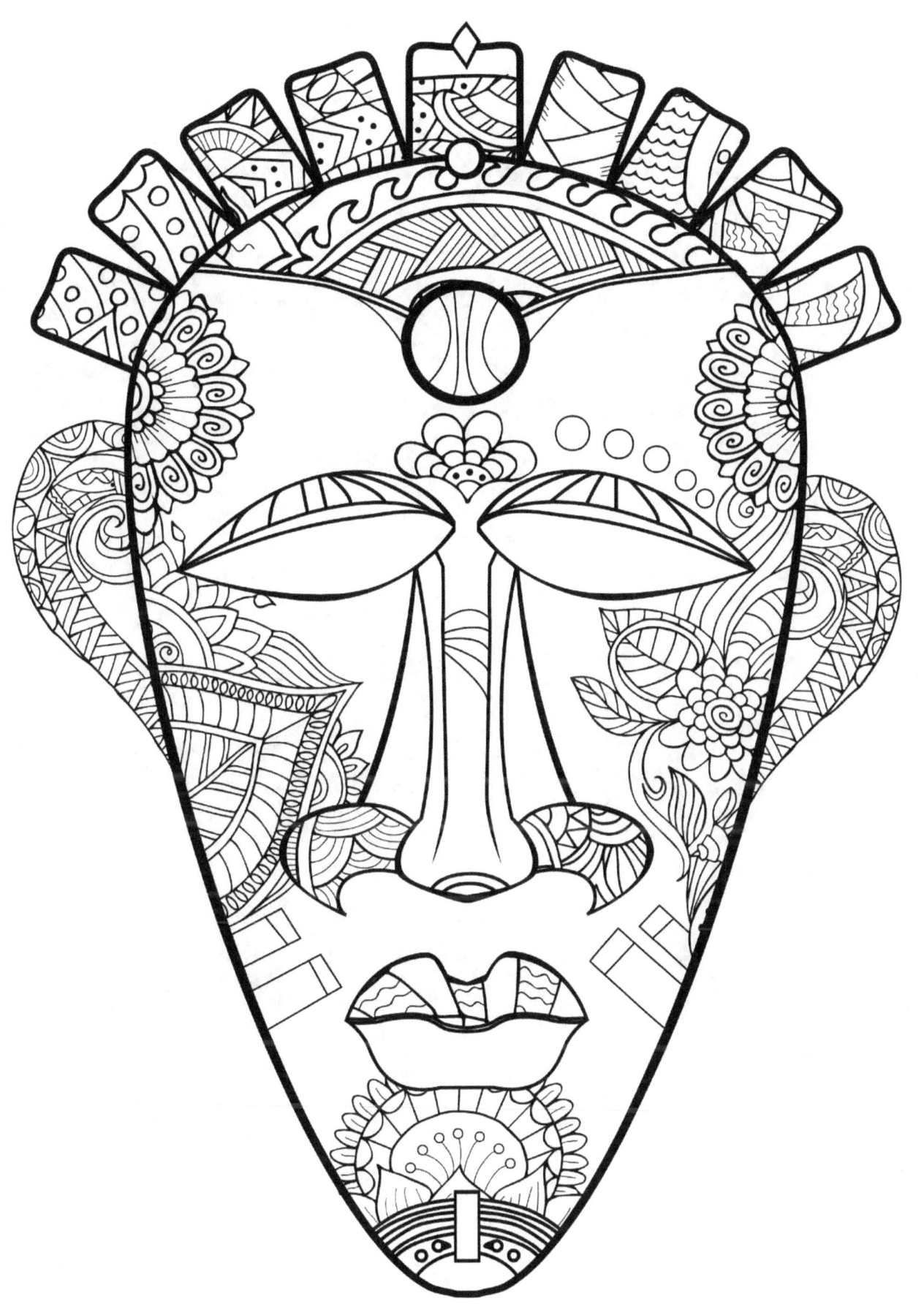

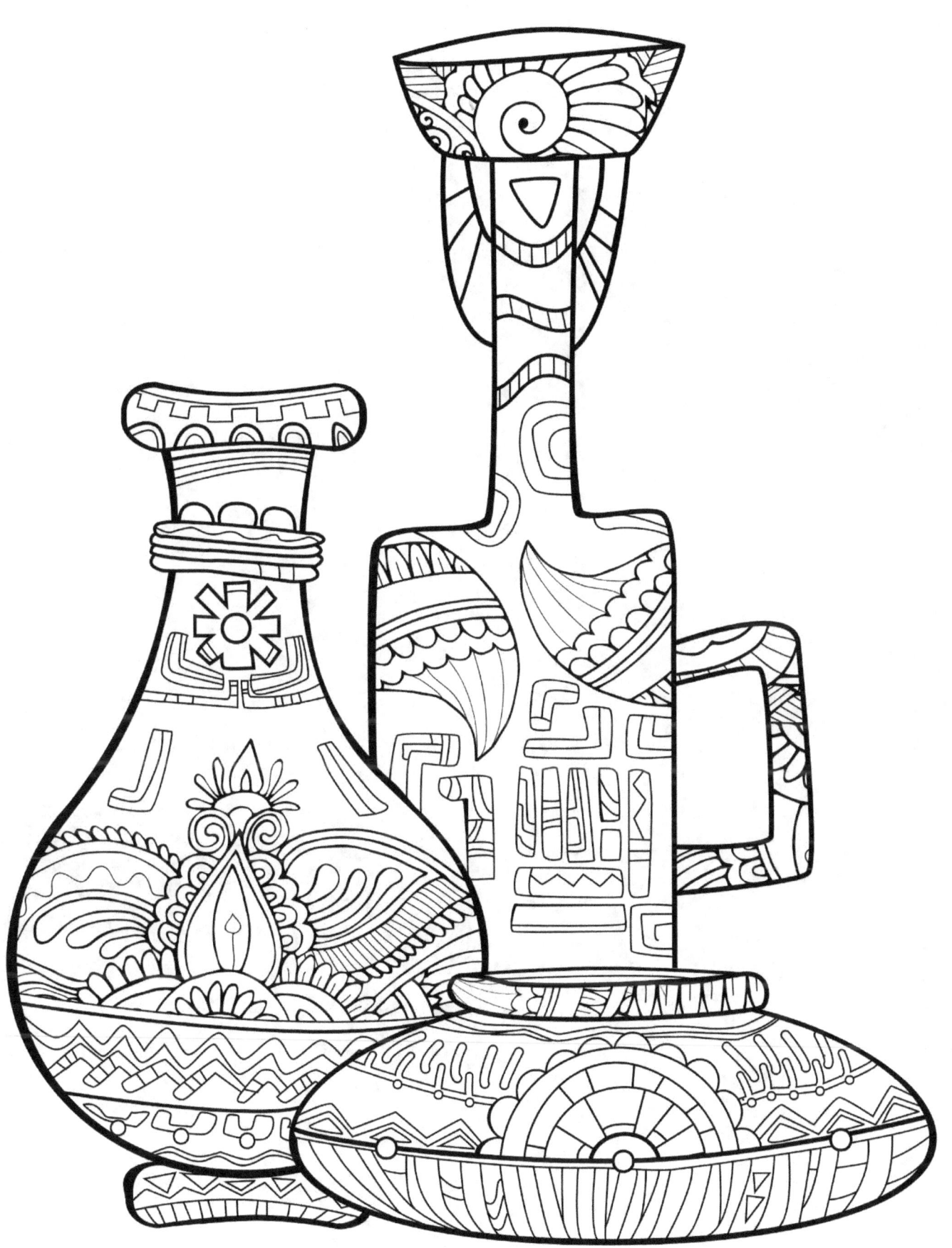

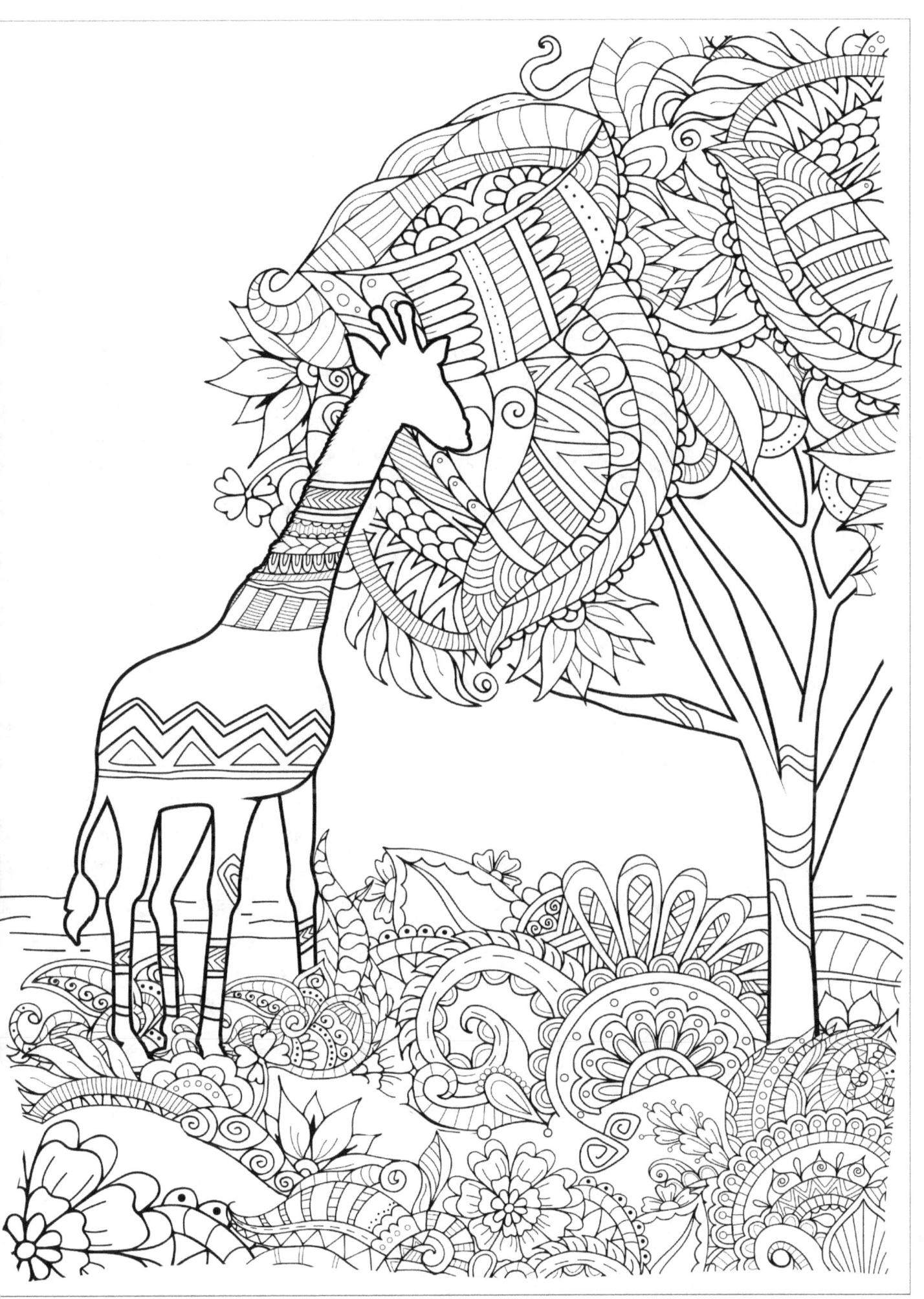

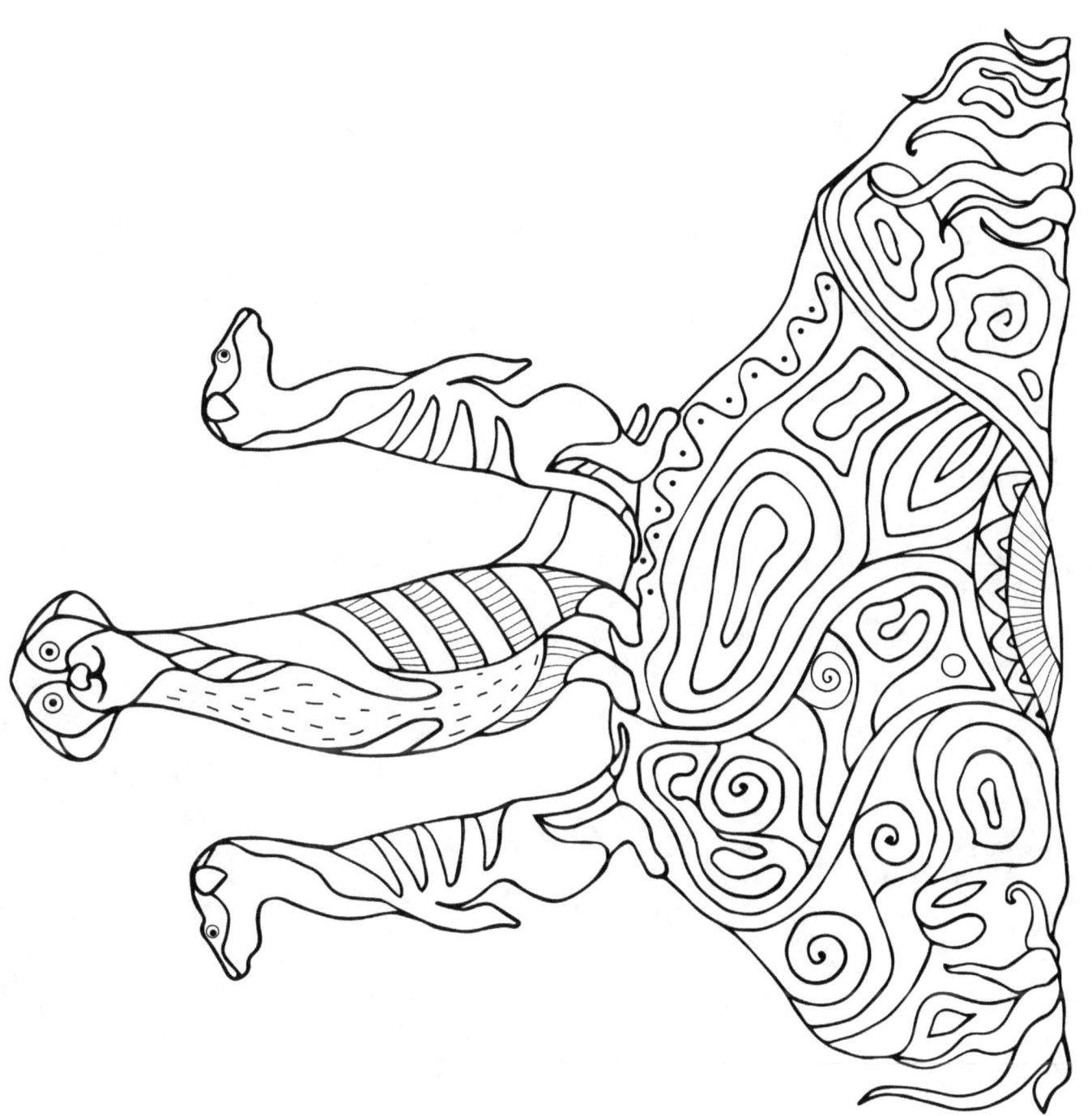

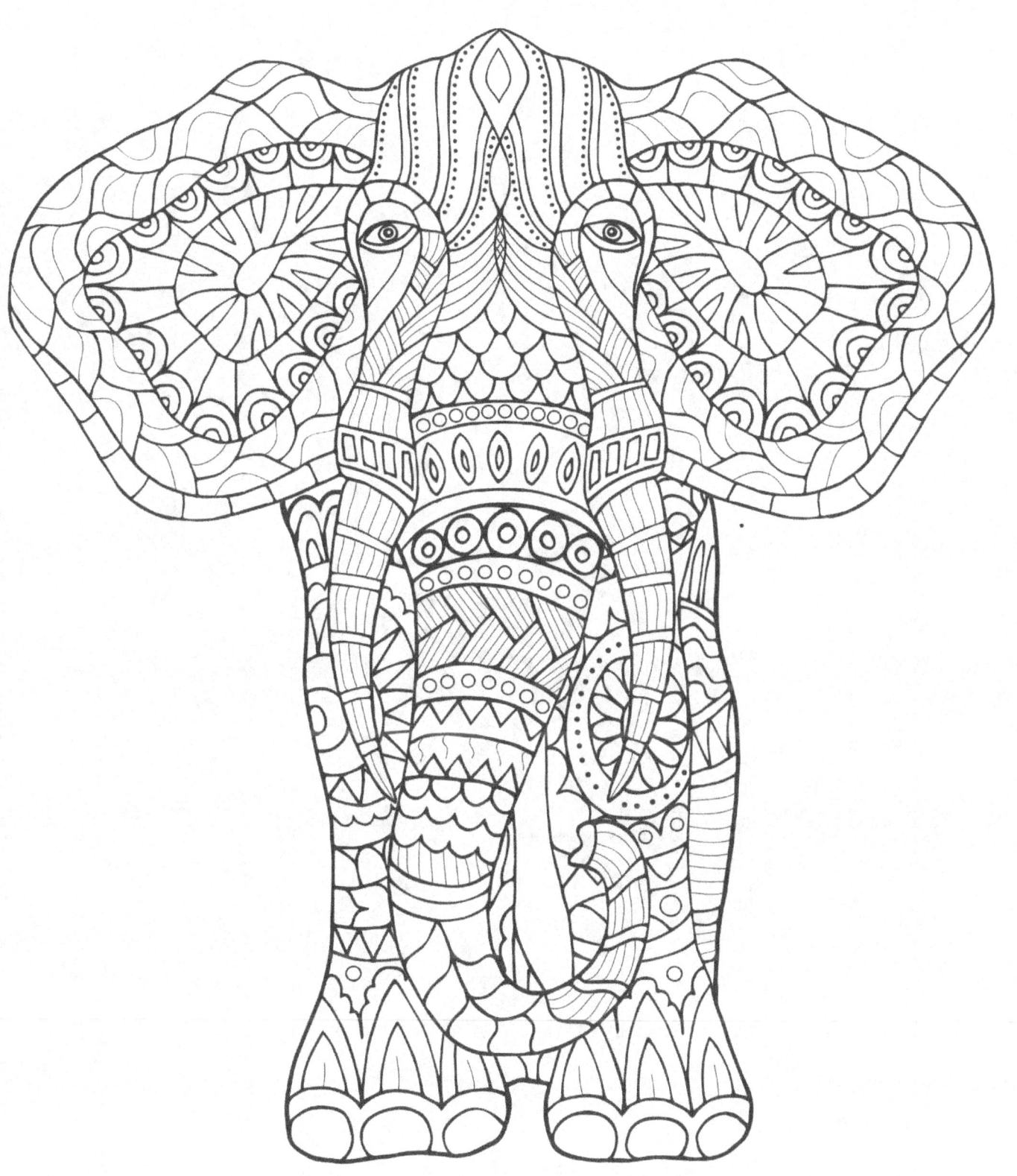

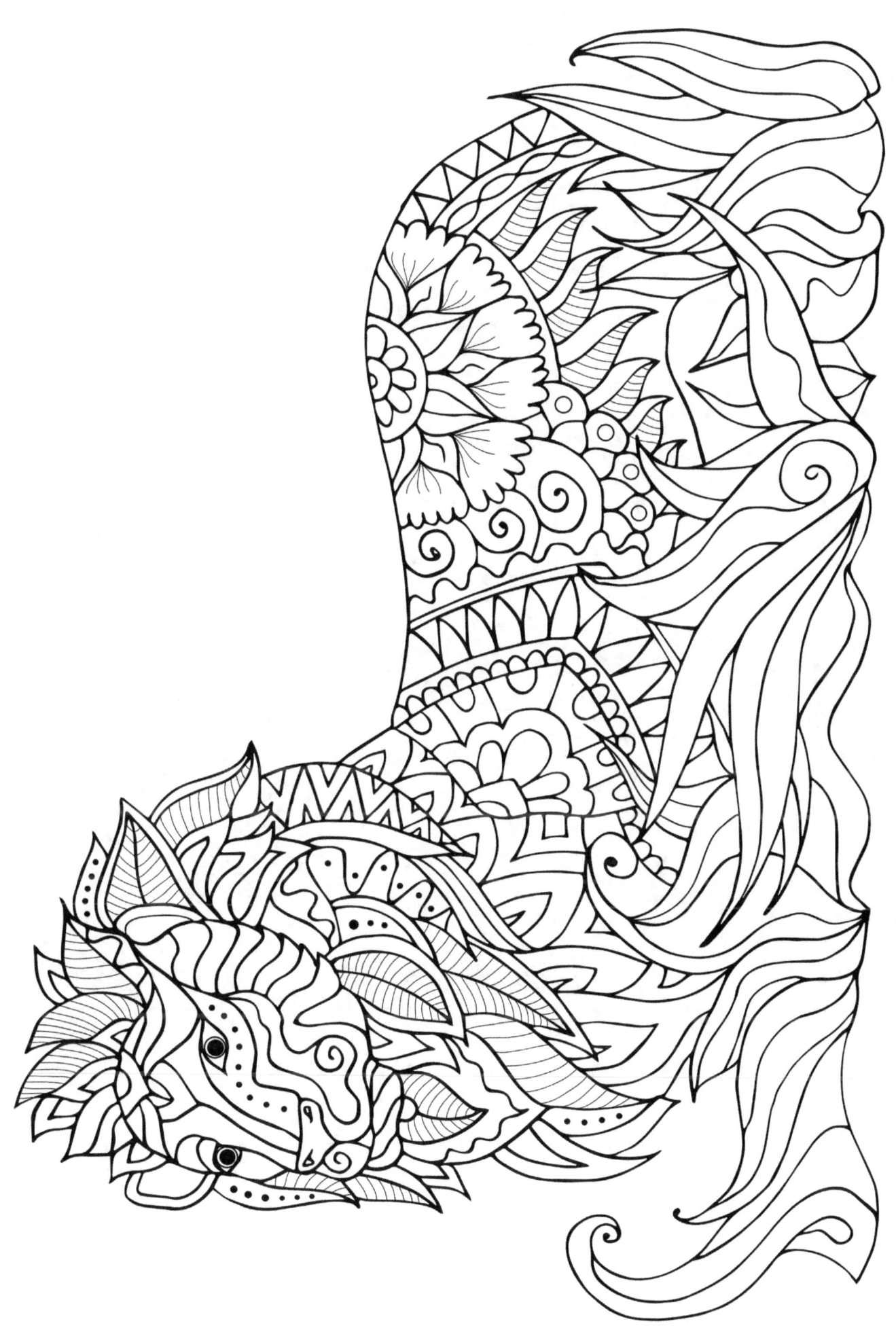

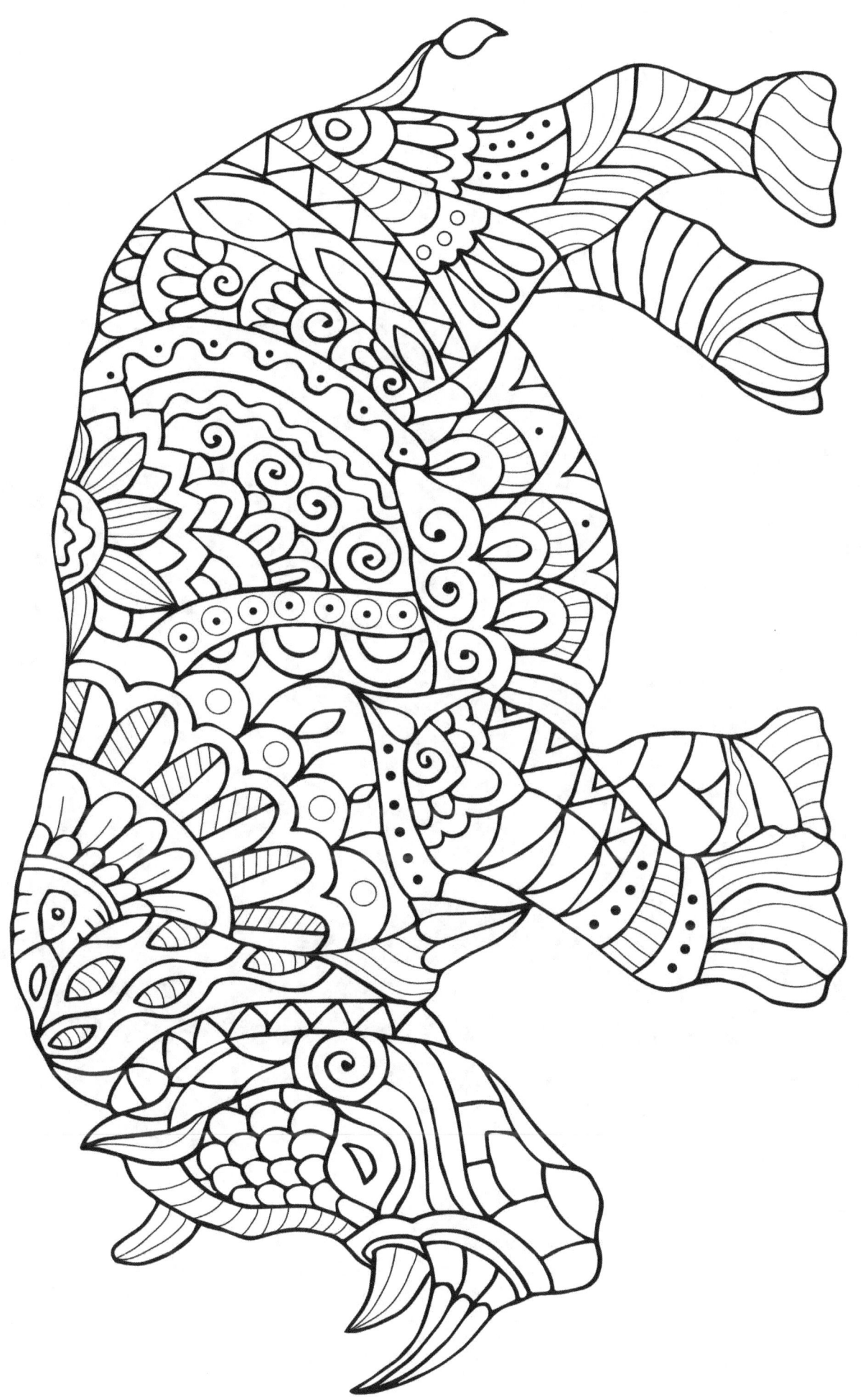

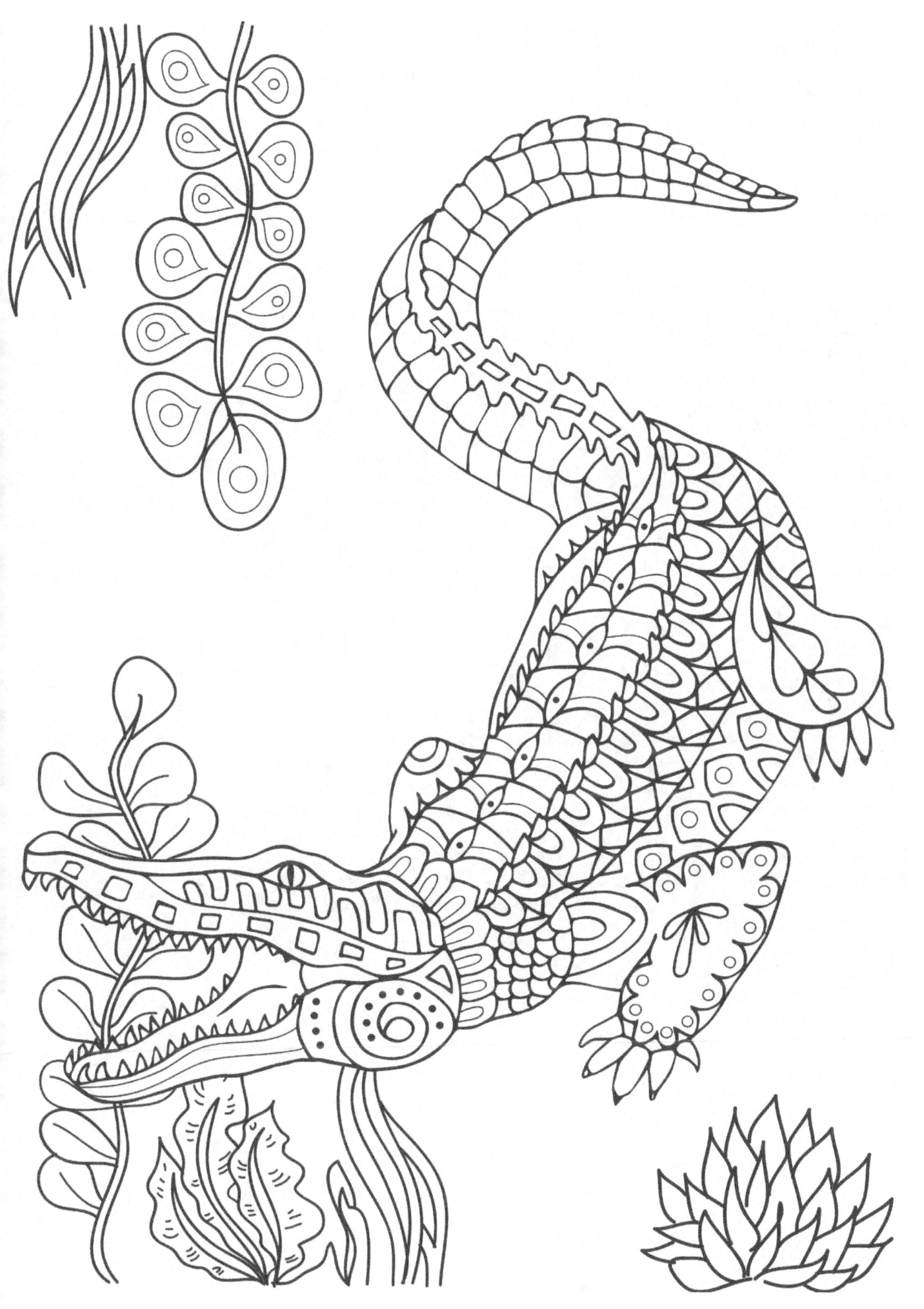

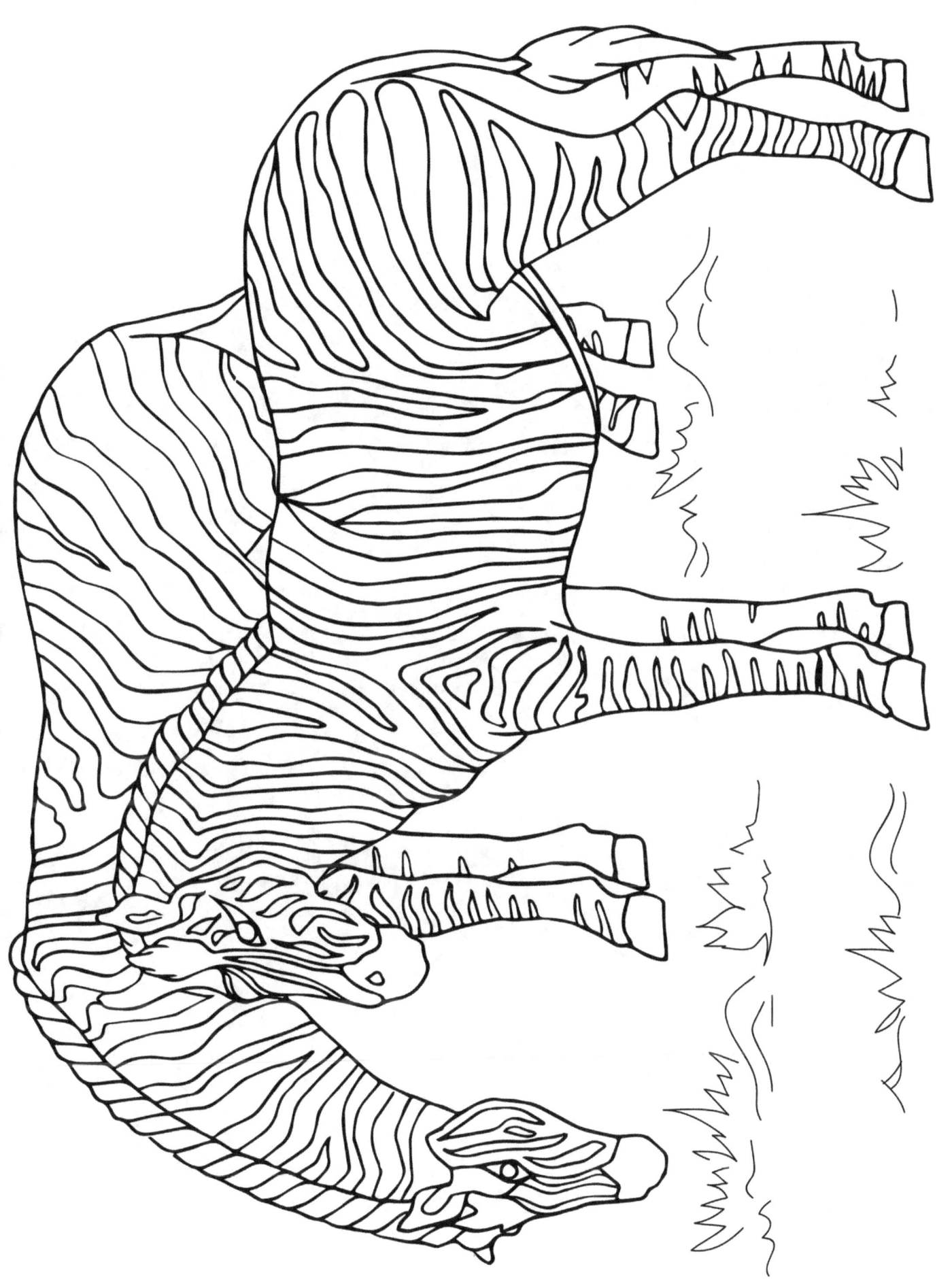

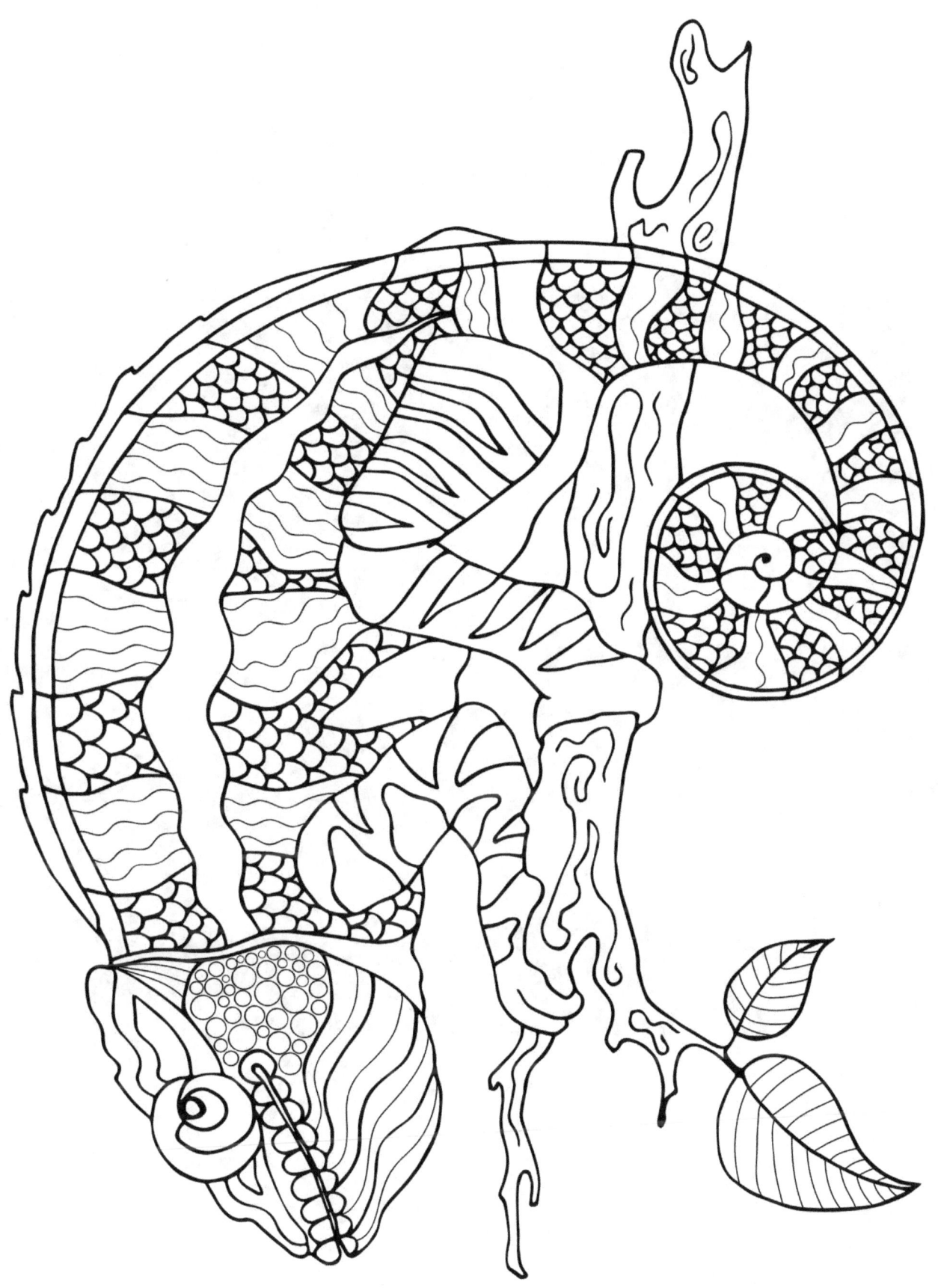

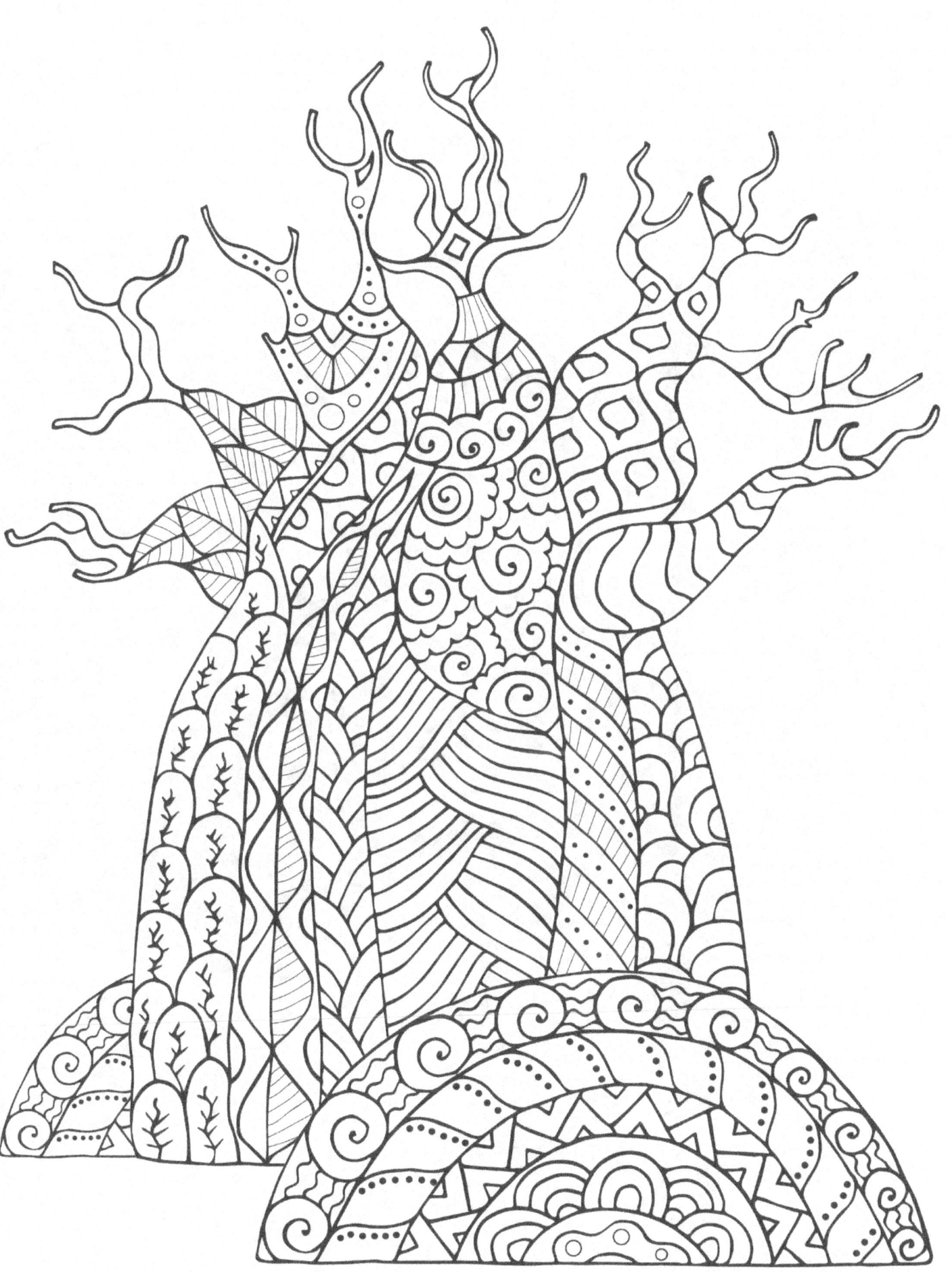

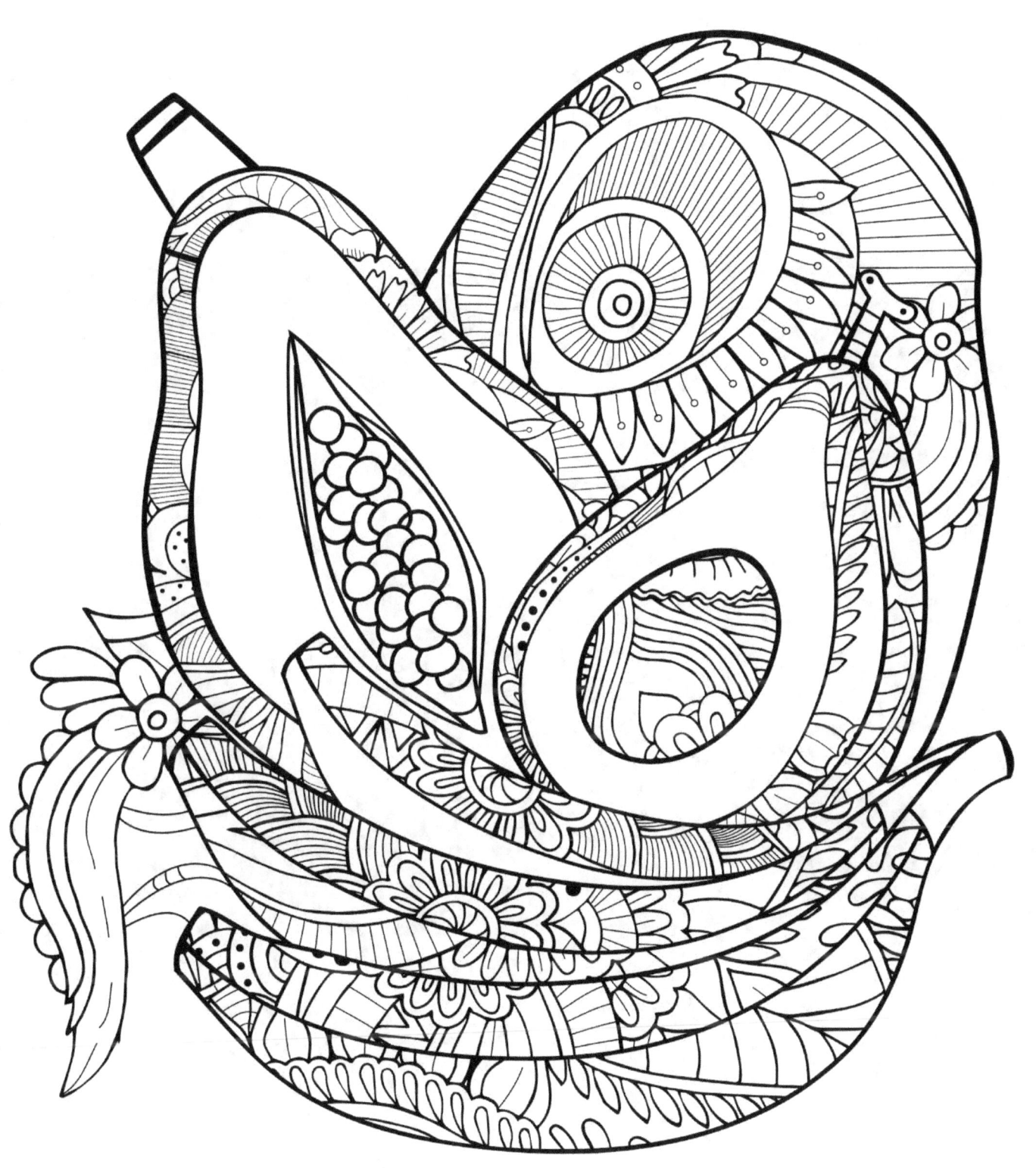

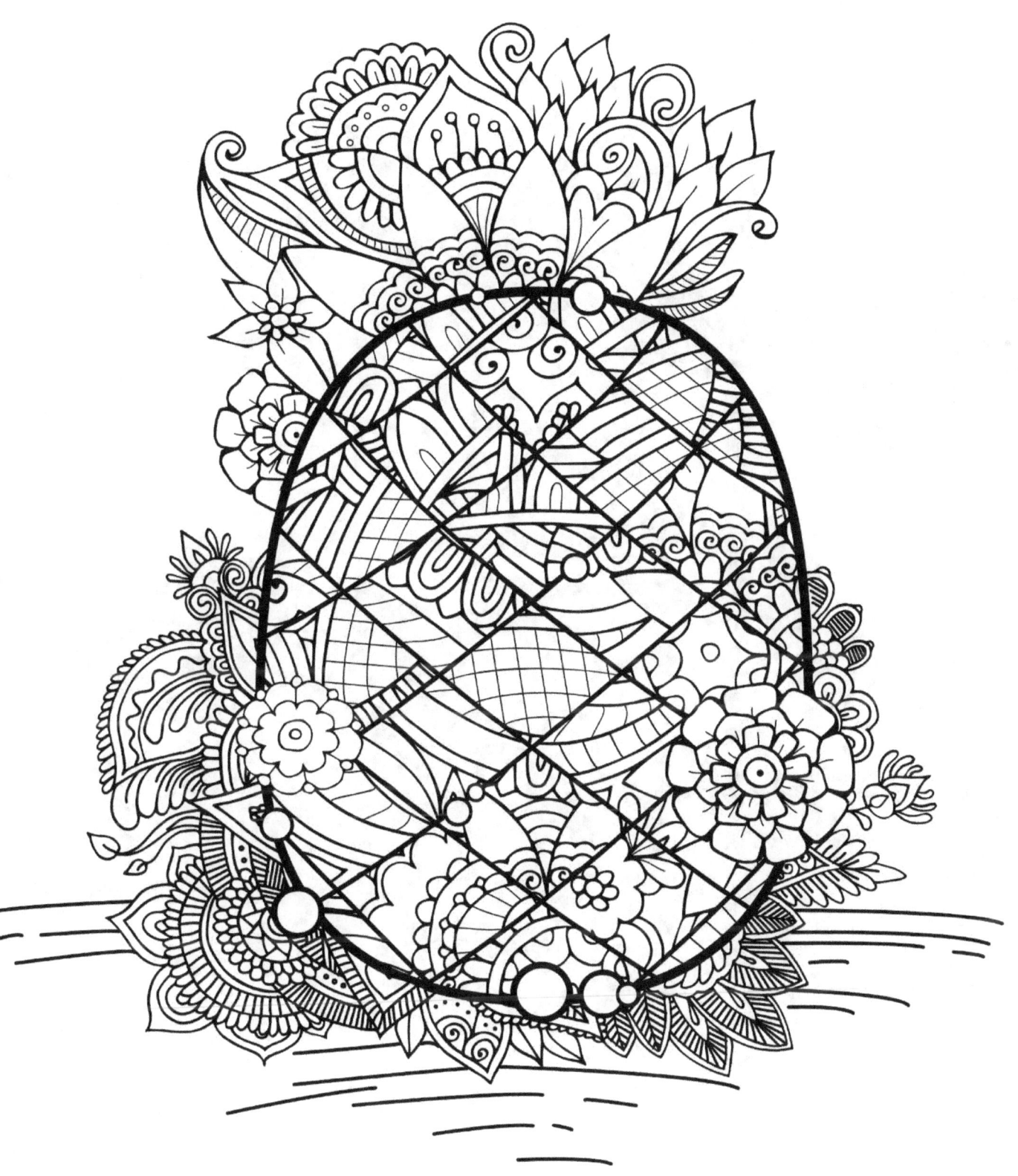

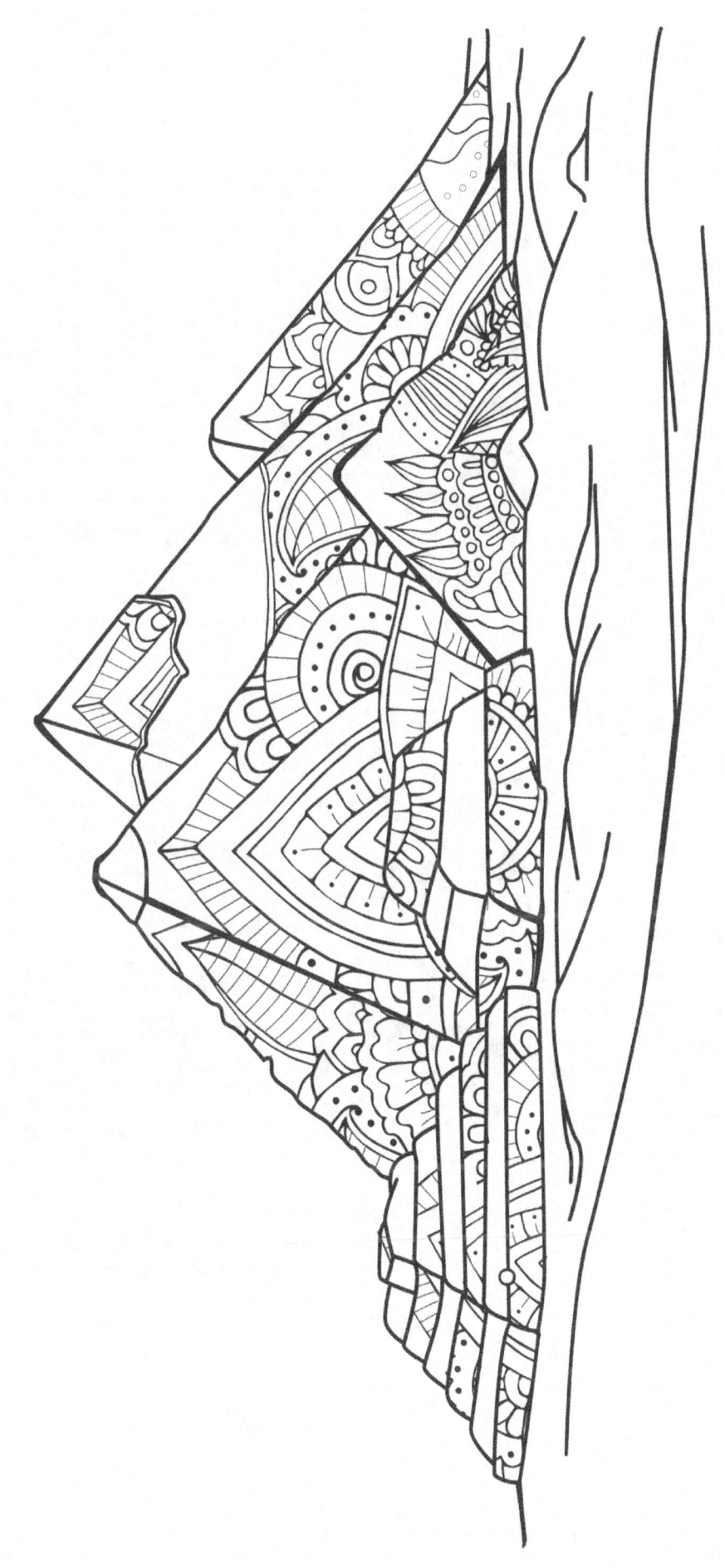

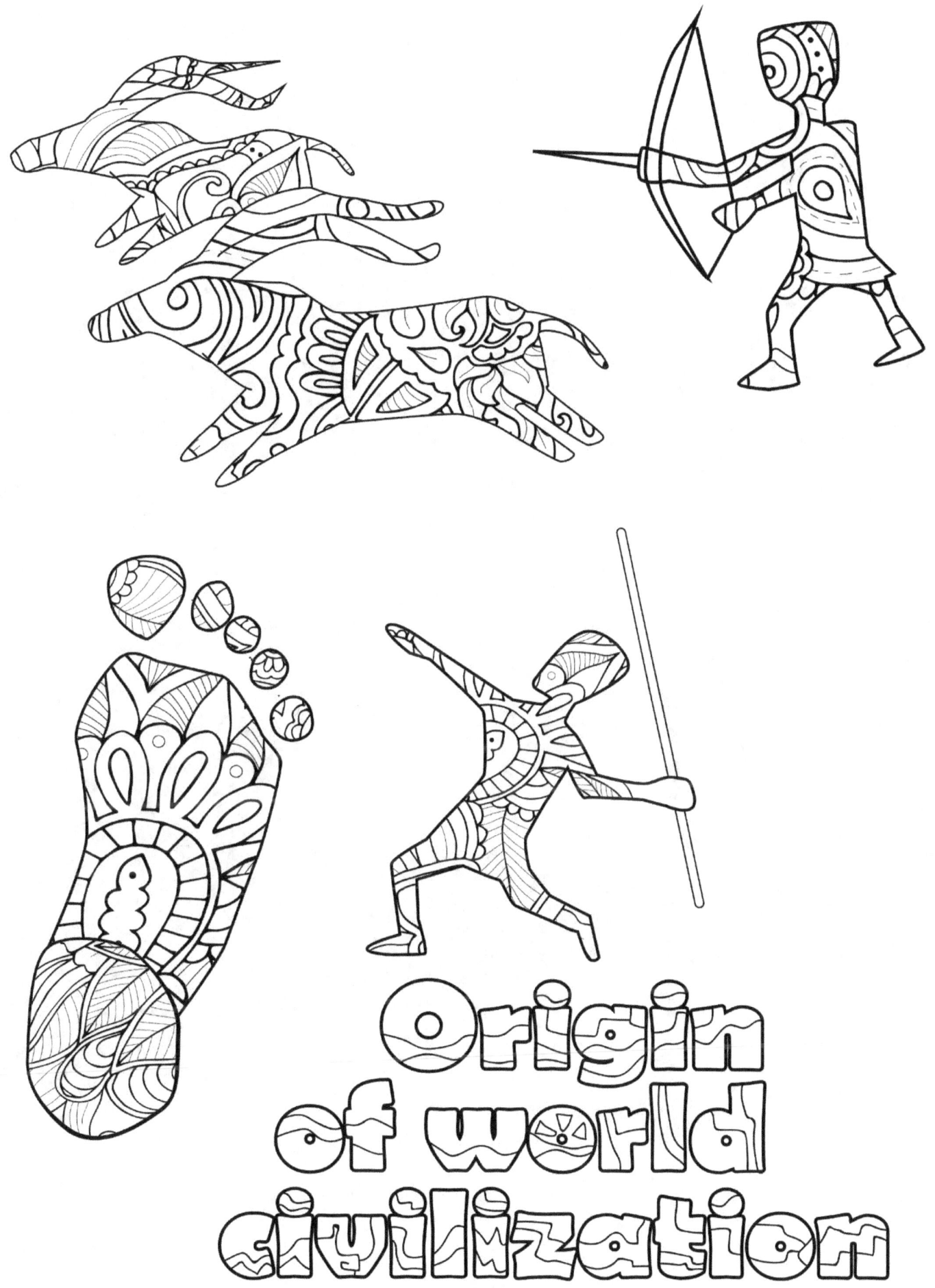

Origin of world civilization

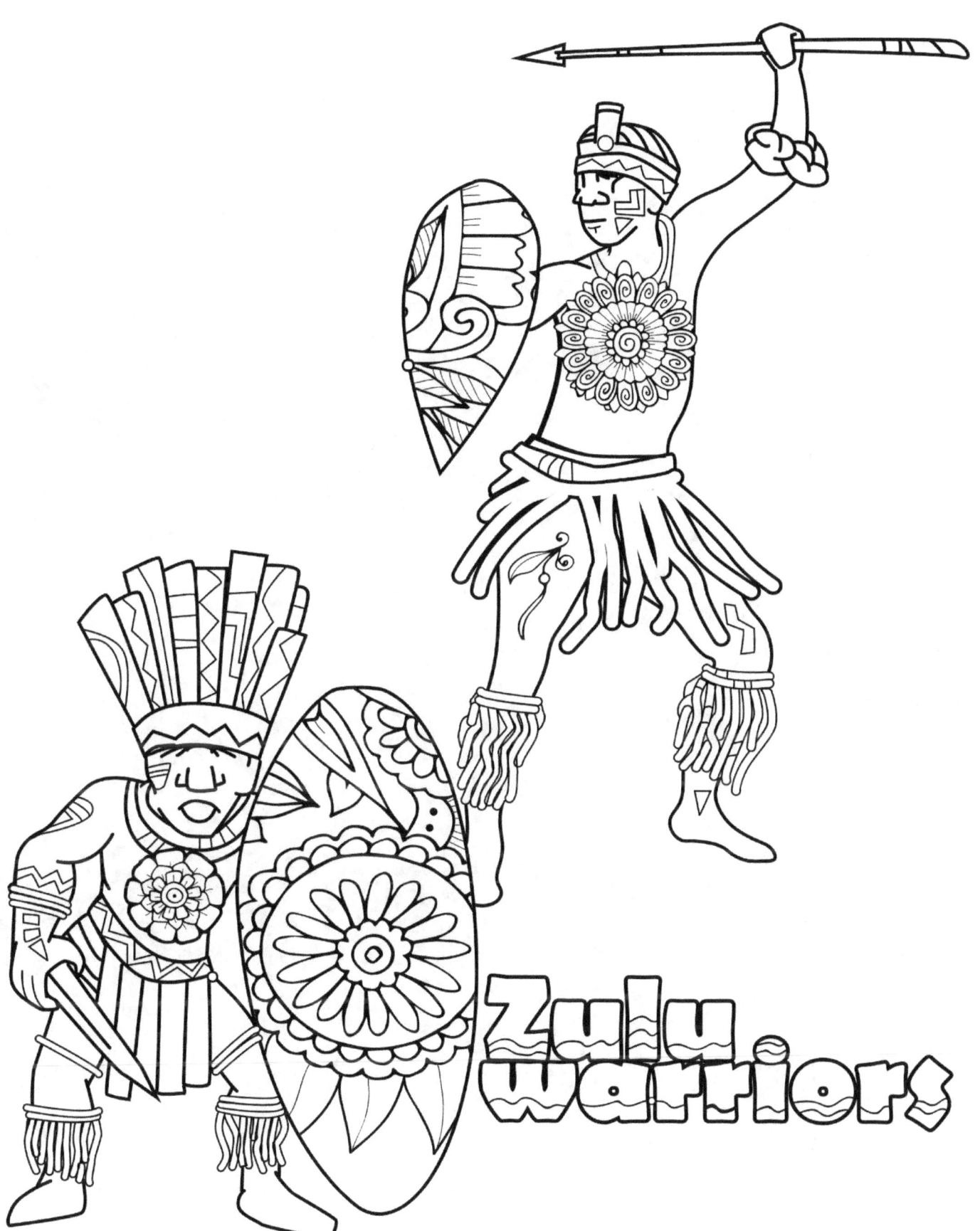

Zulu warriors

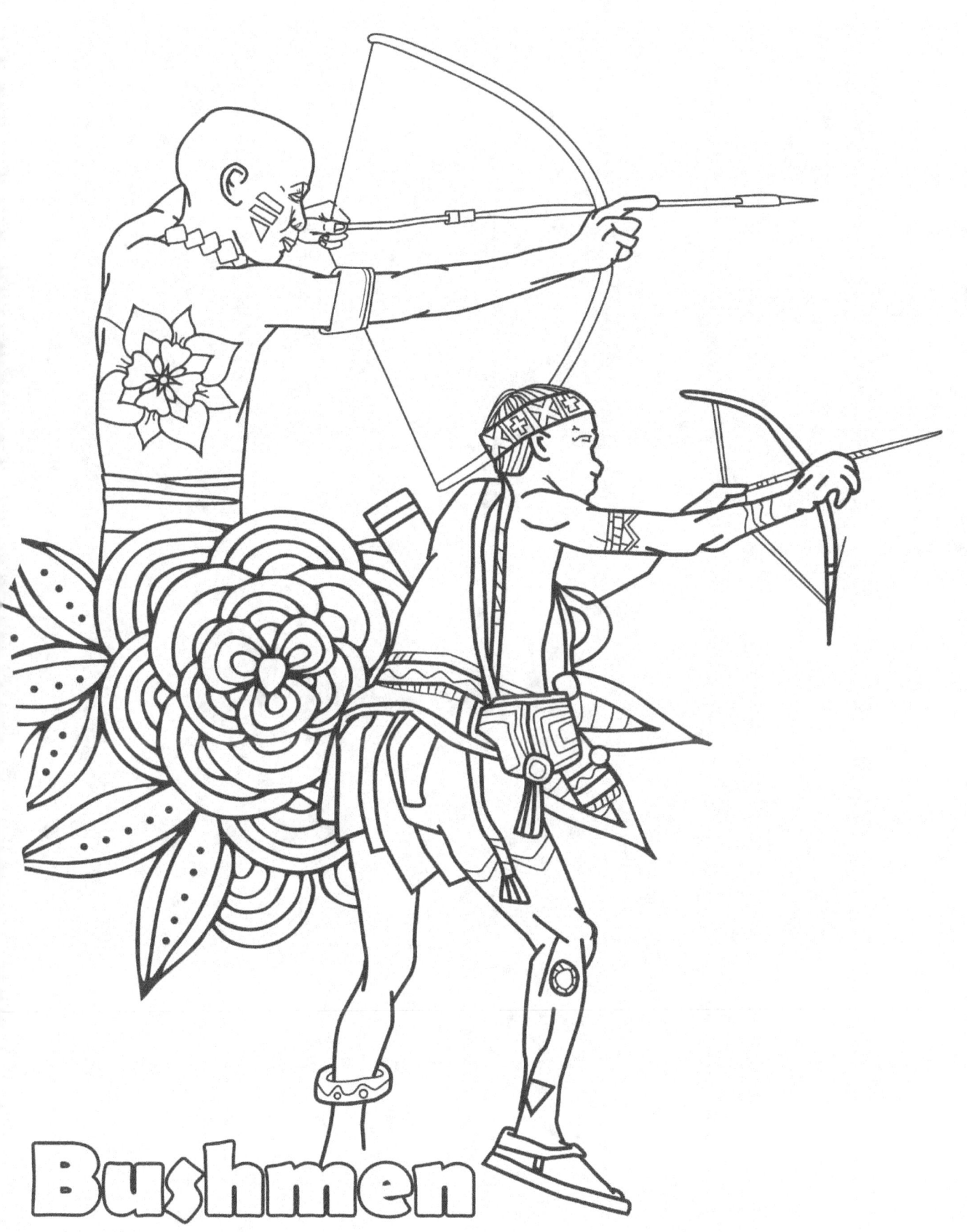

Bushmen

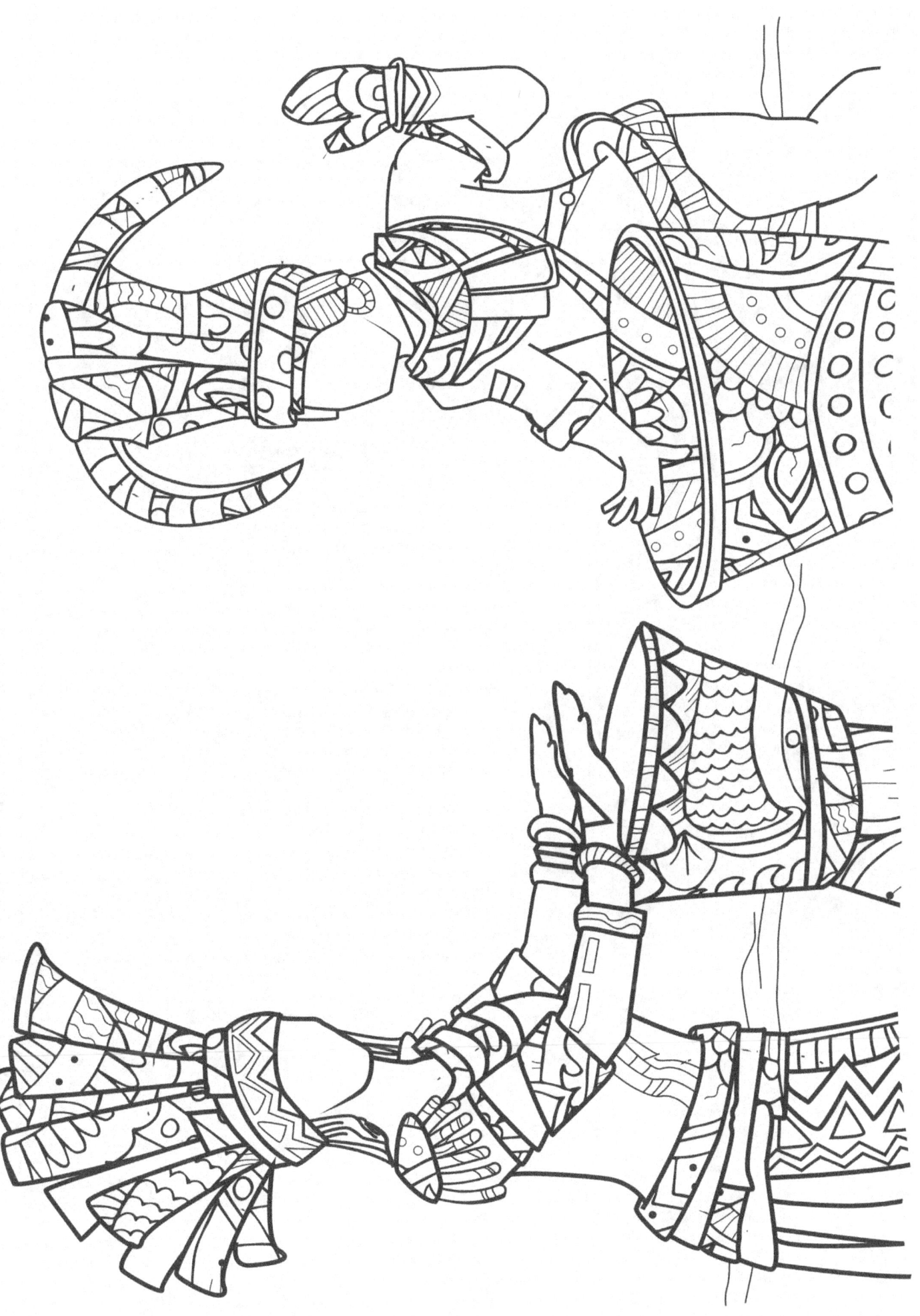

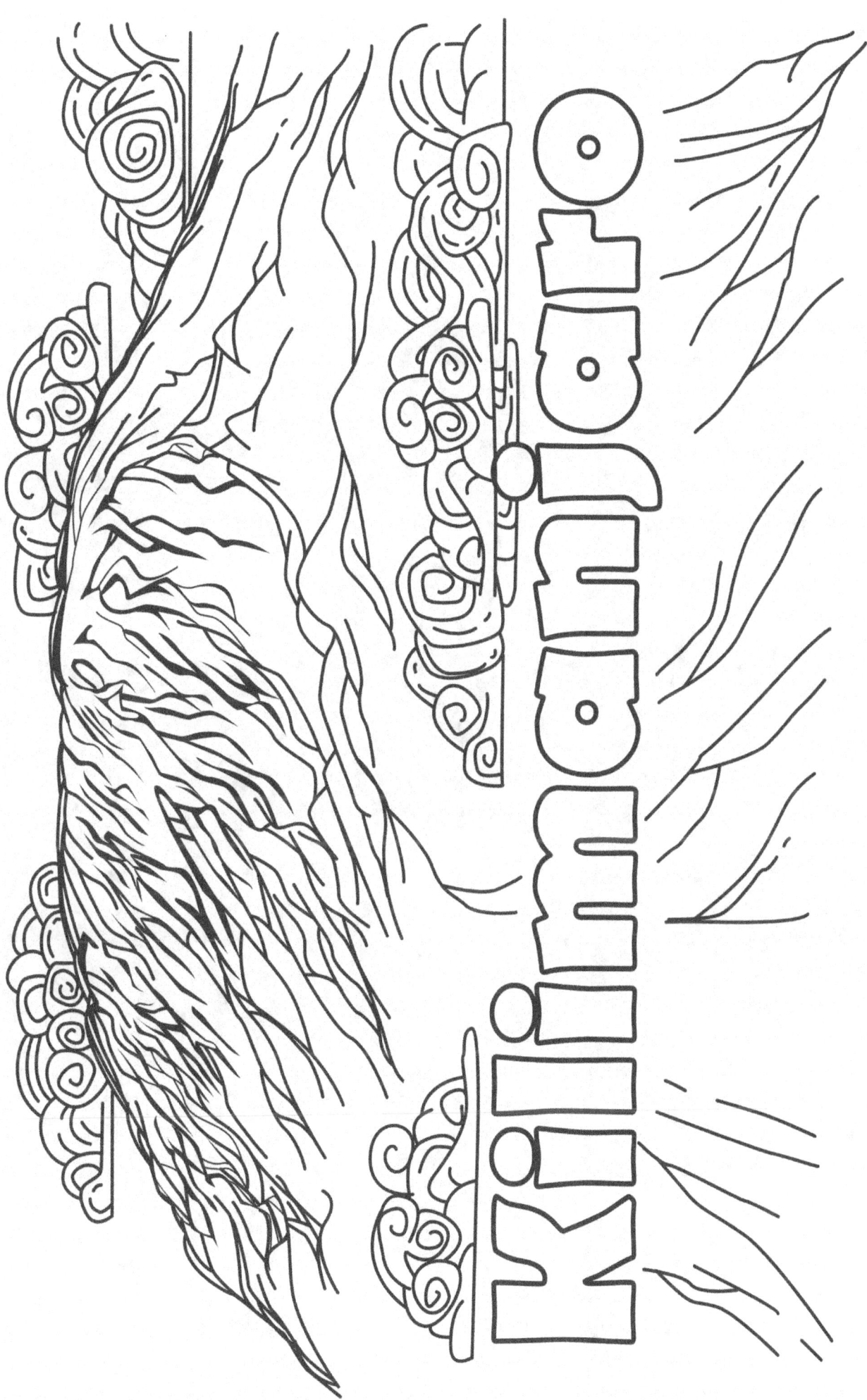

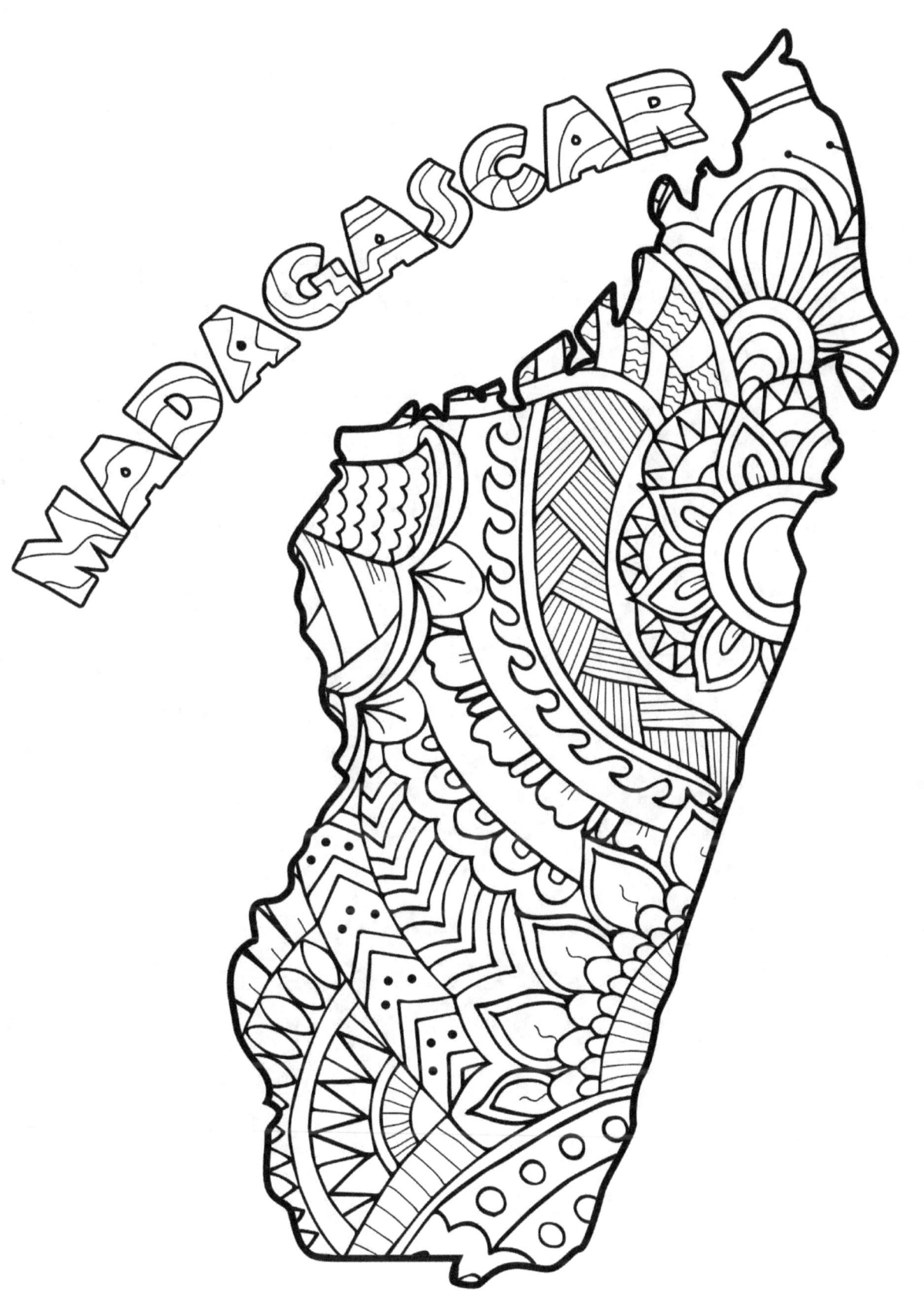

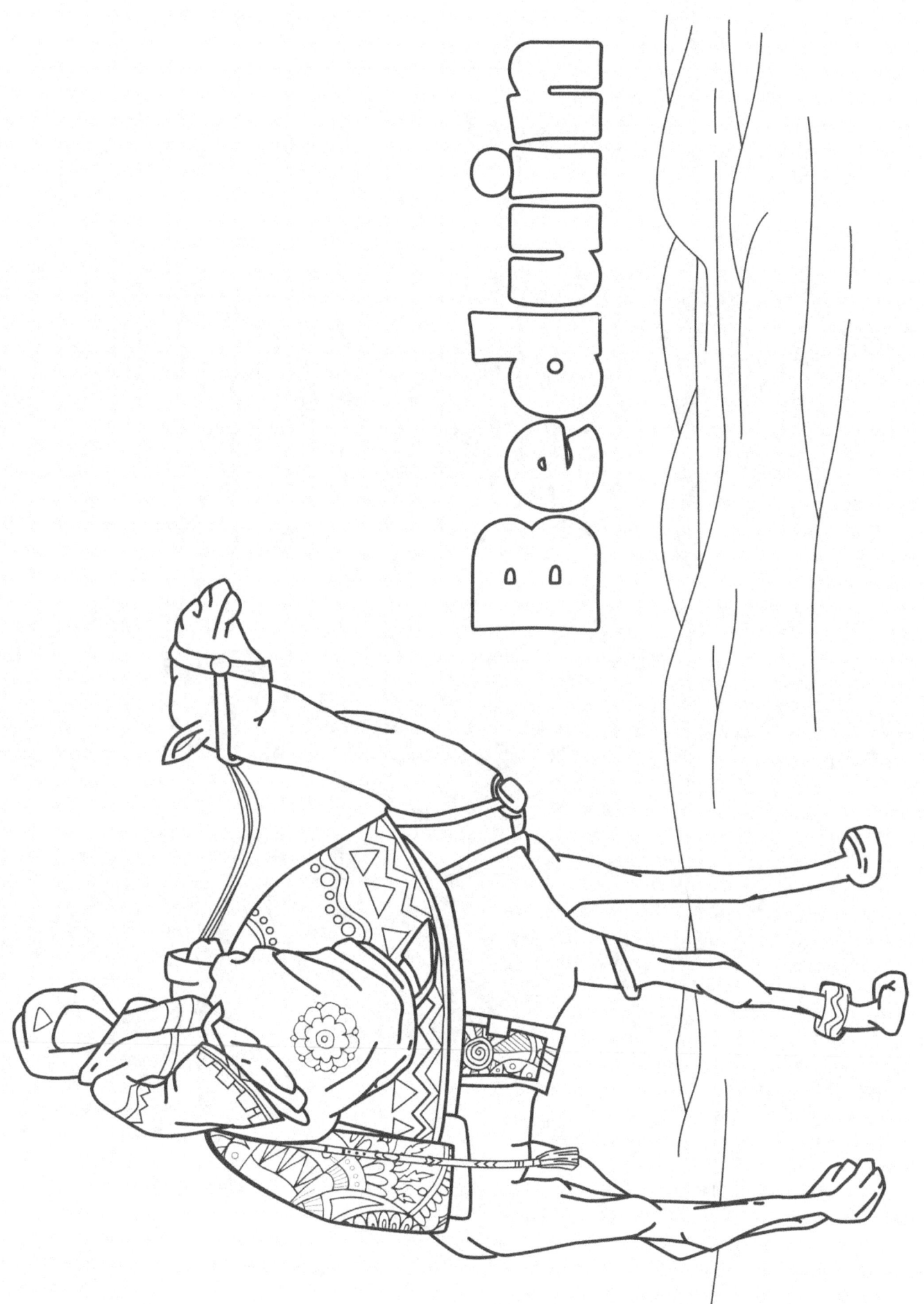

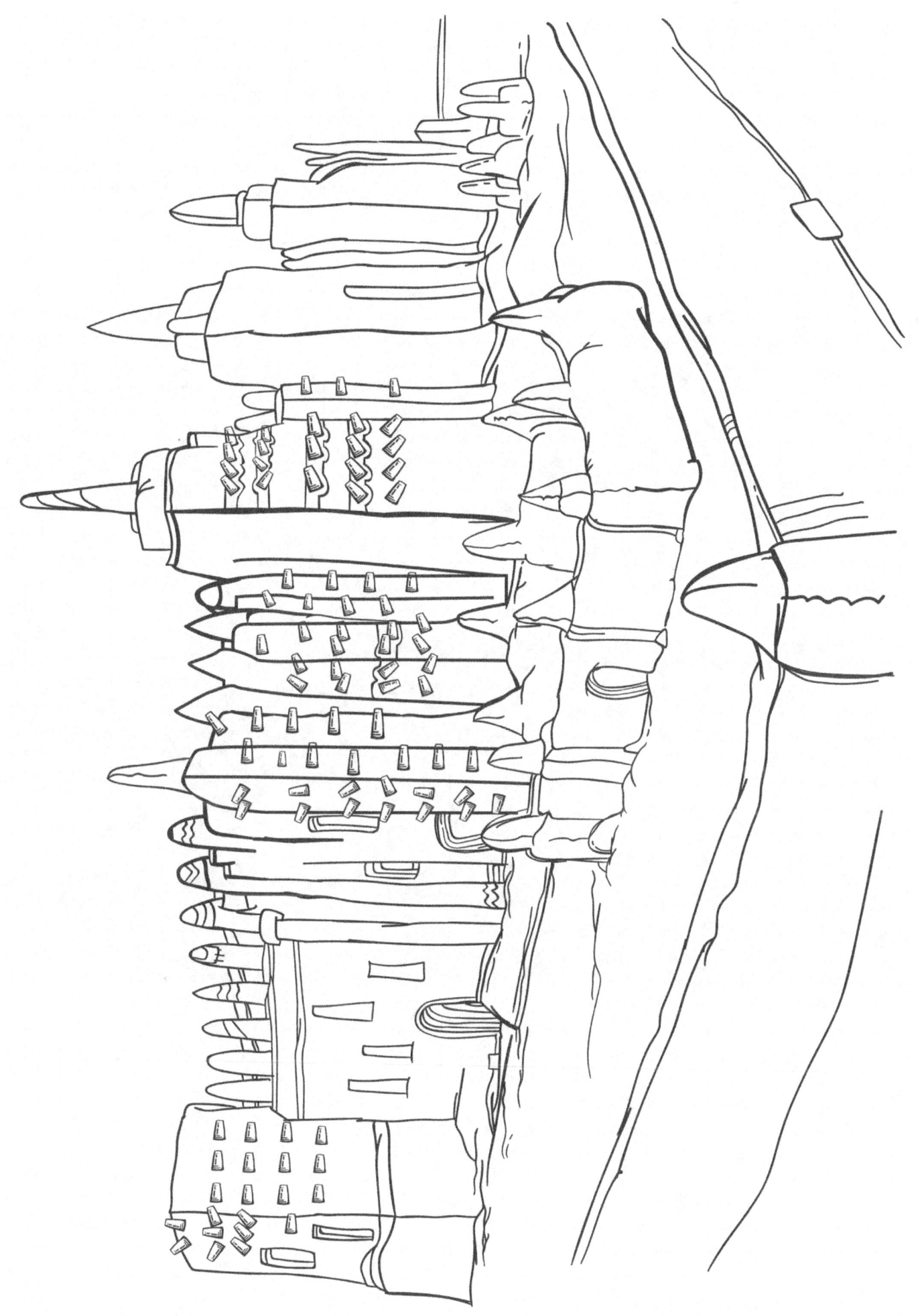

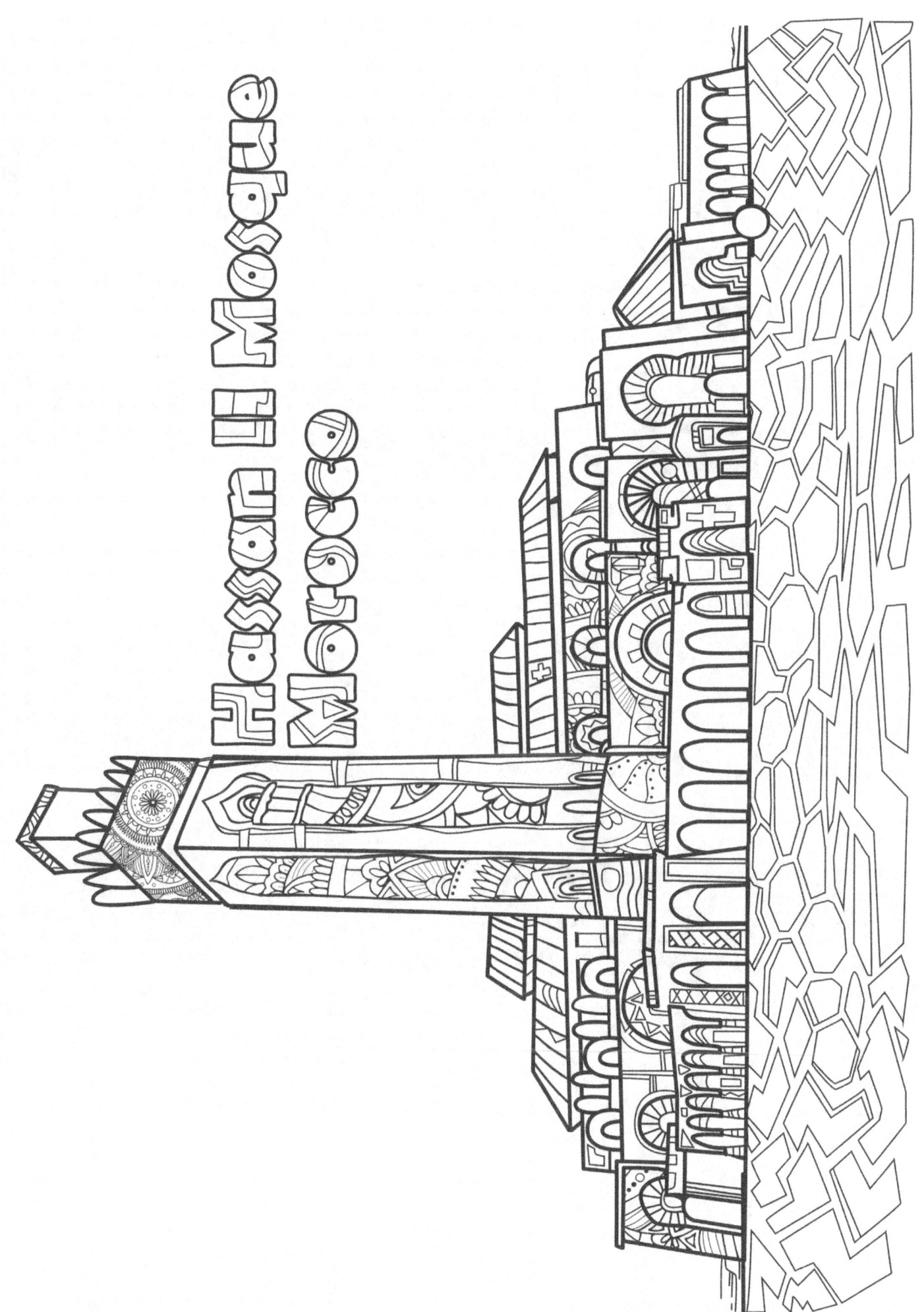

Hassan II Mosque
Morocco

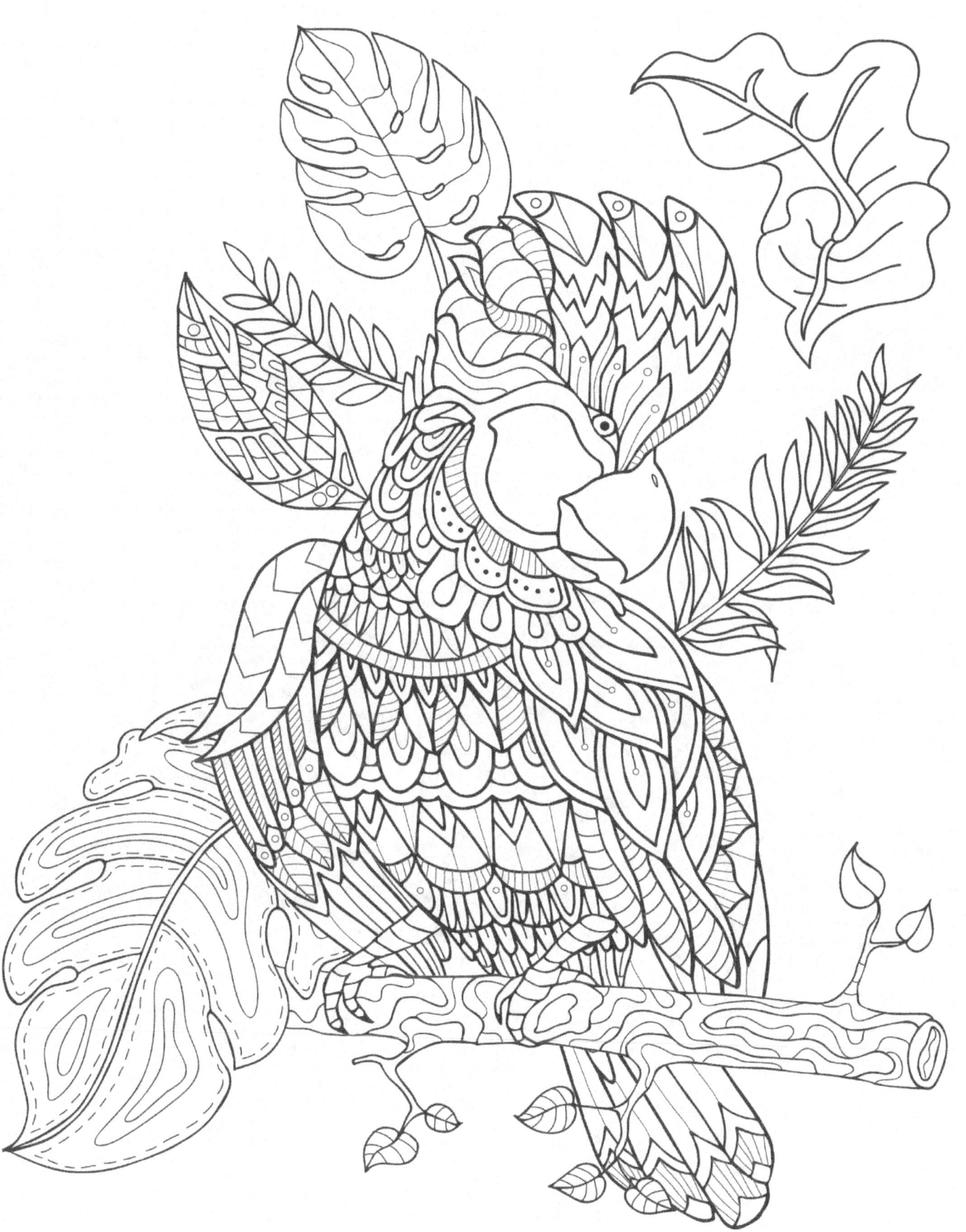

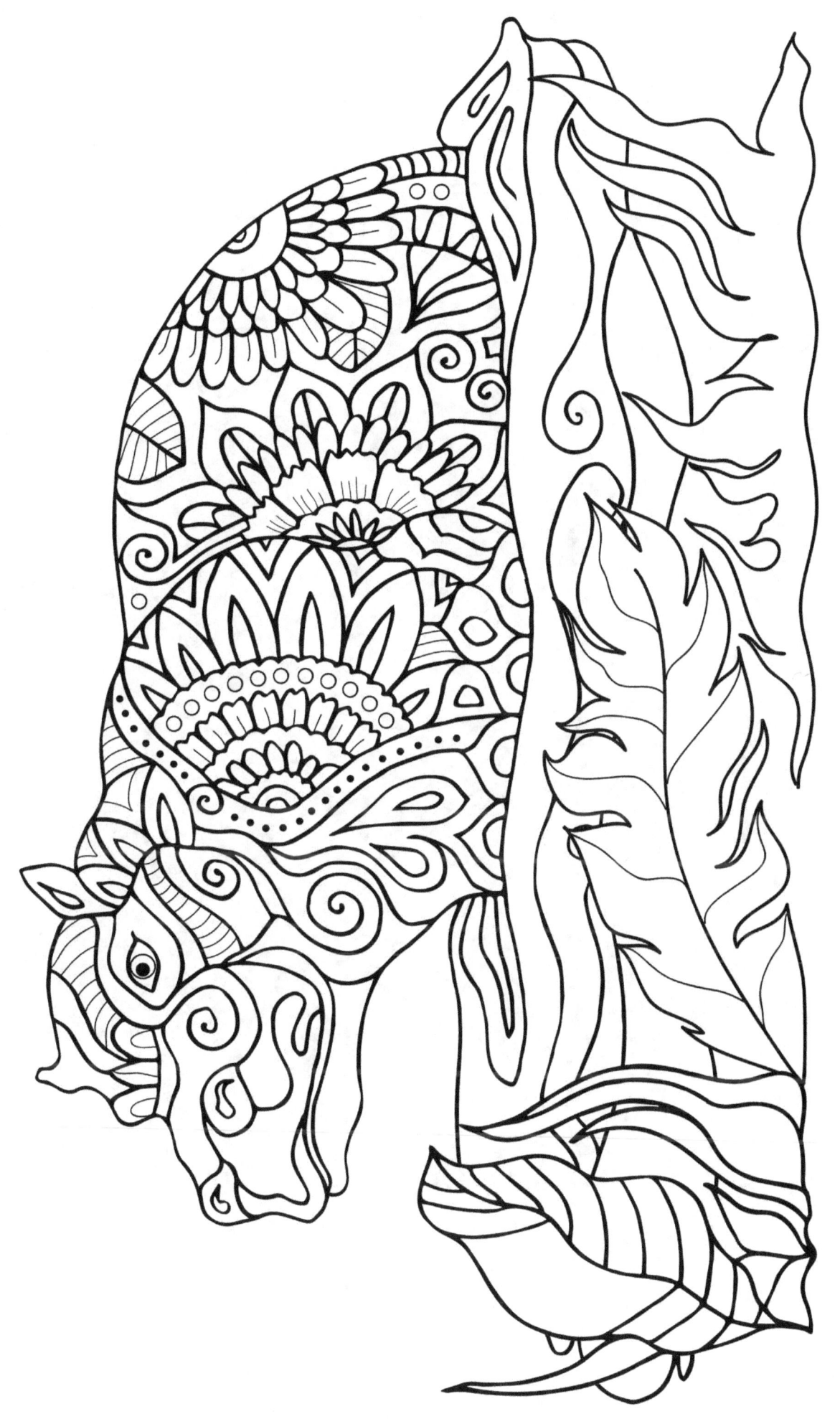

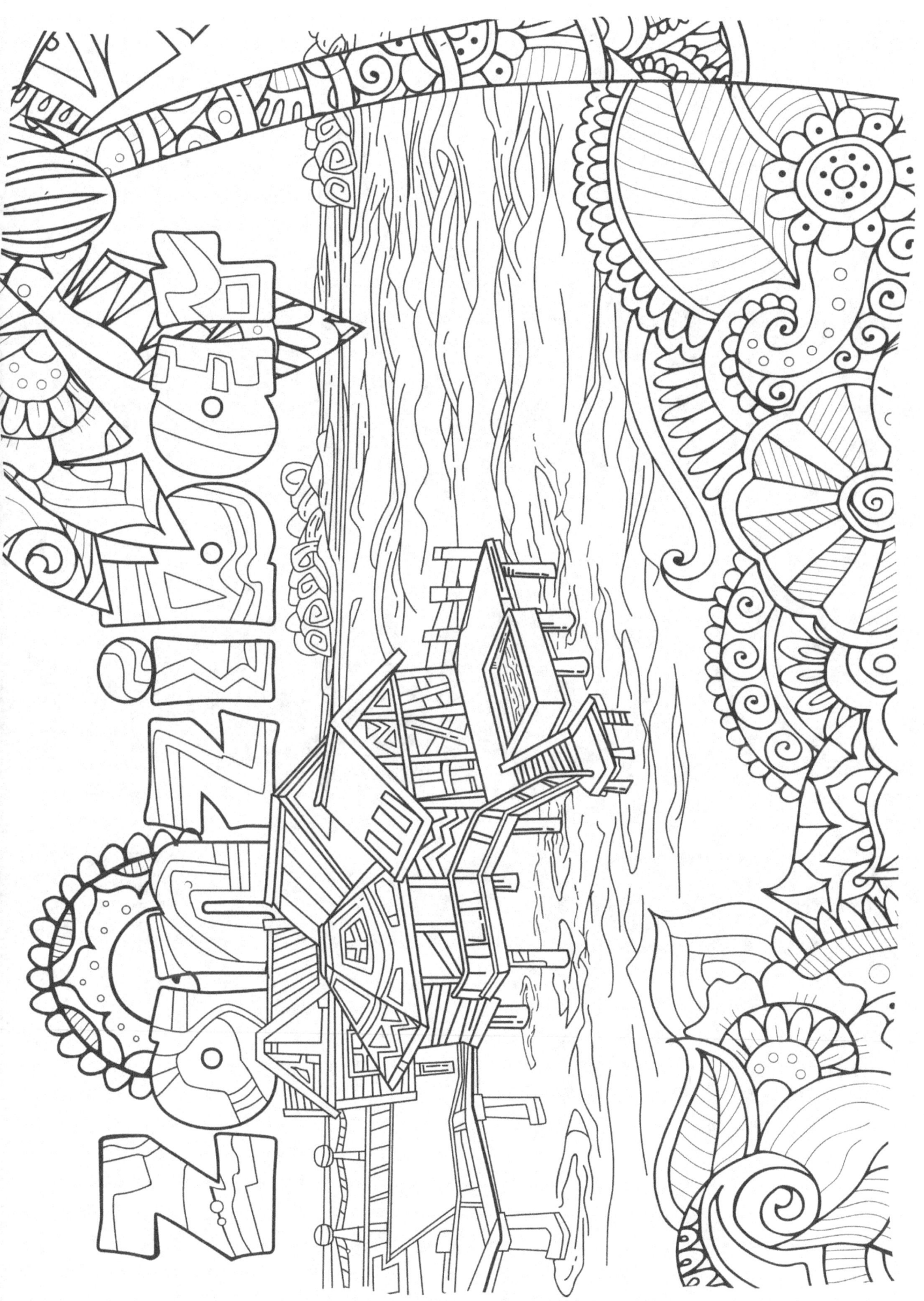

Gods of Egypt

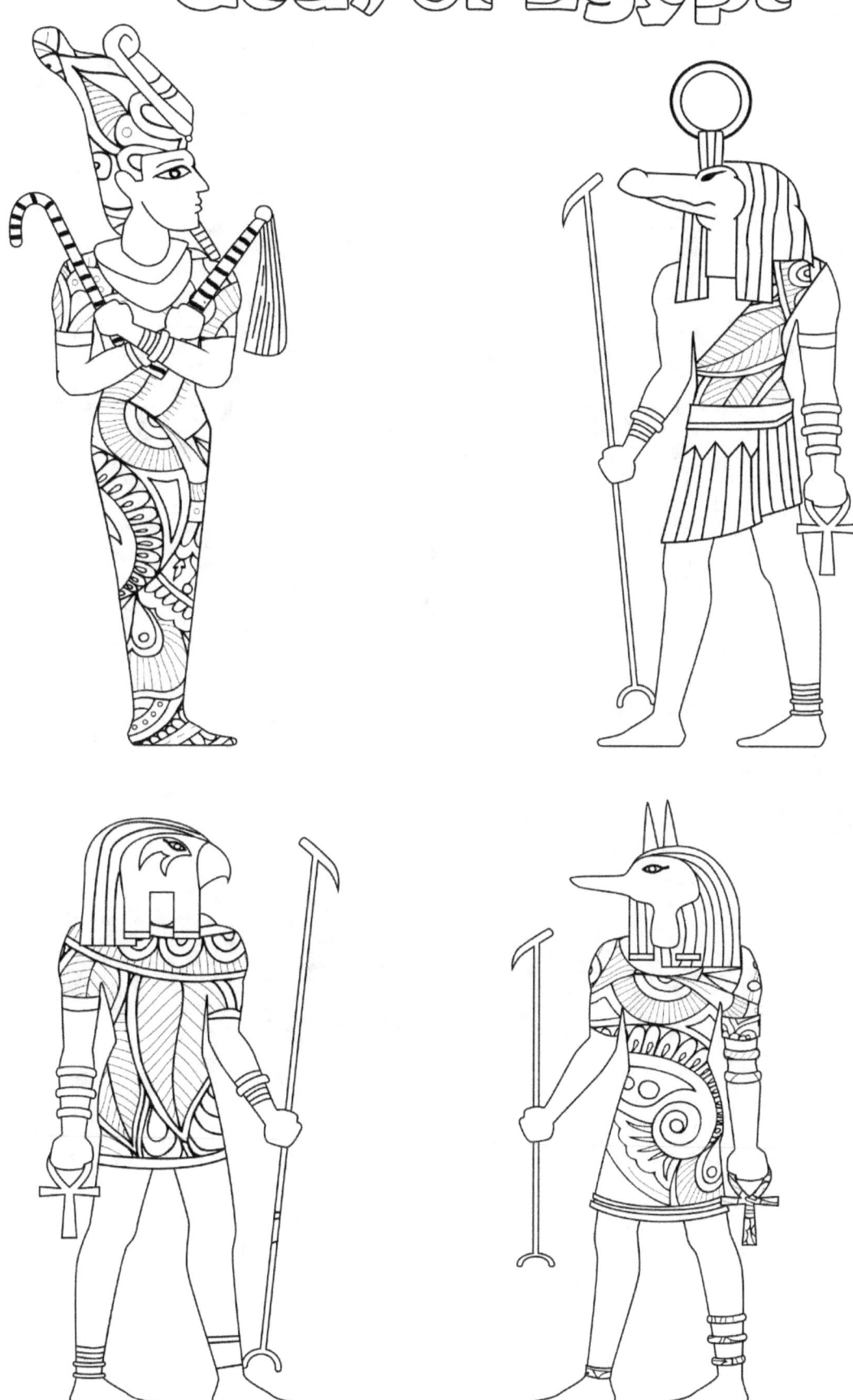

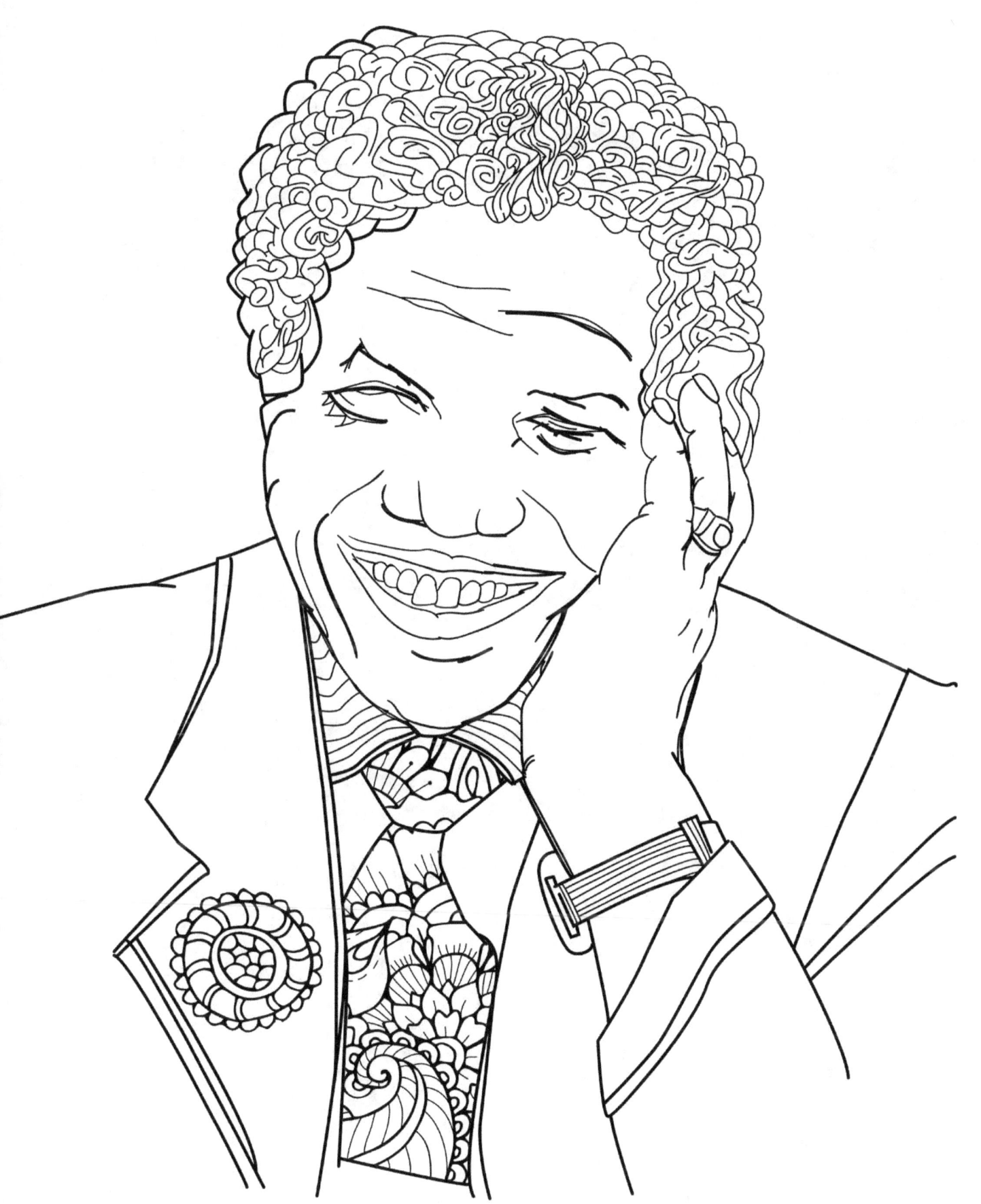

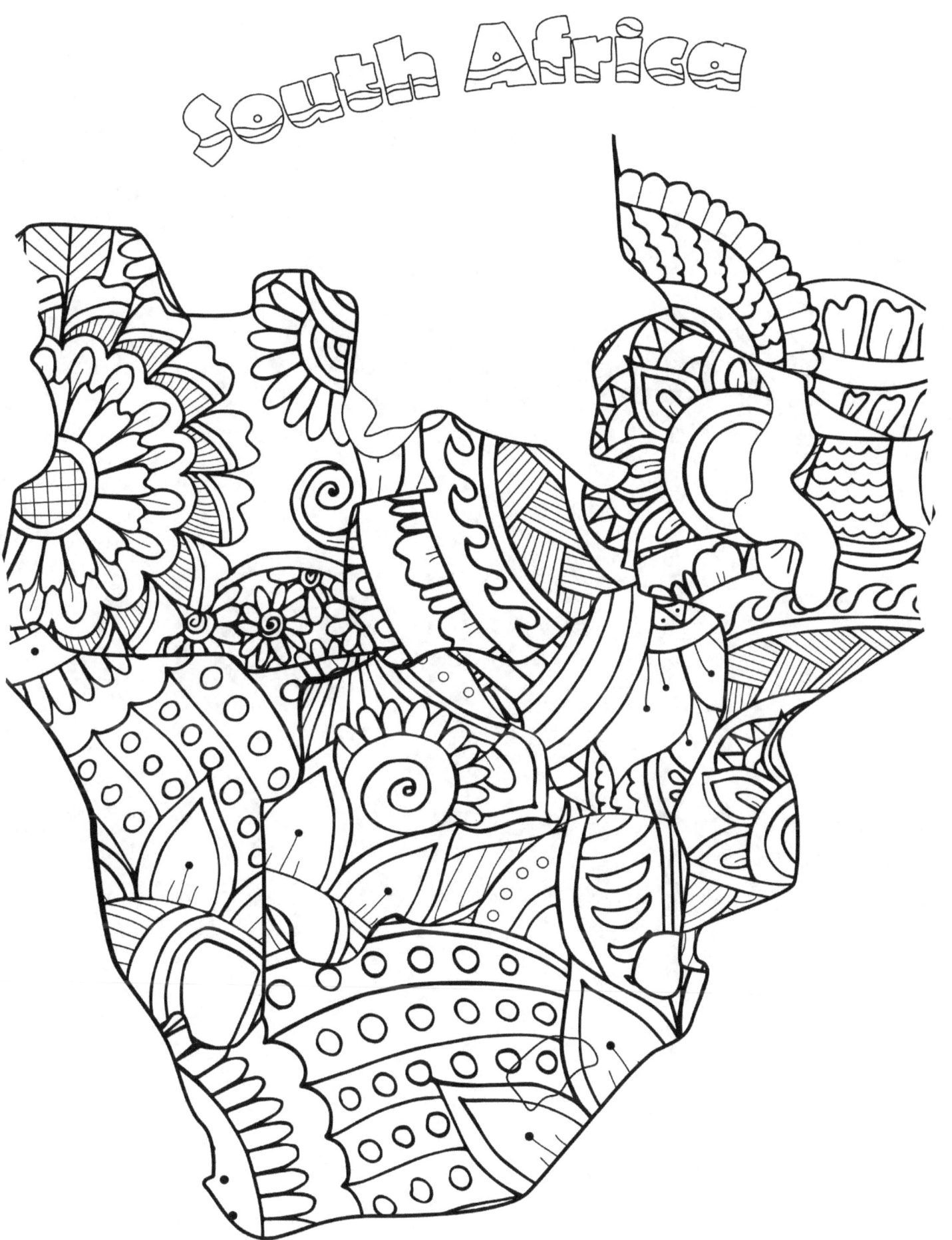

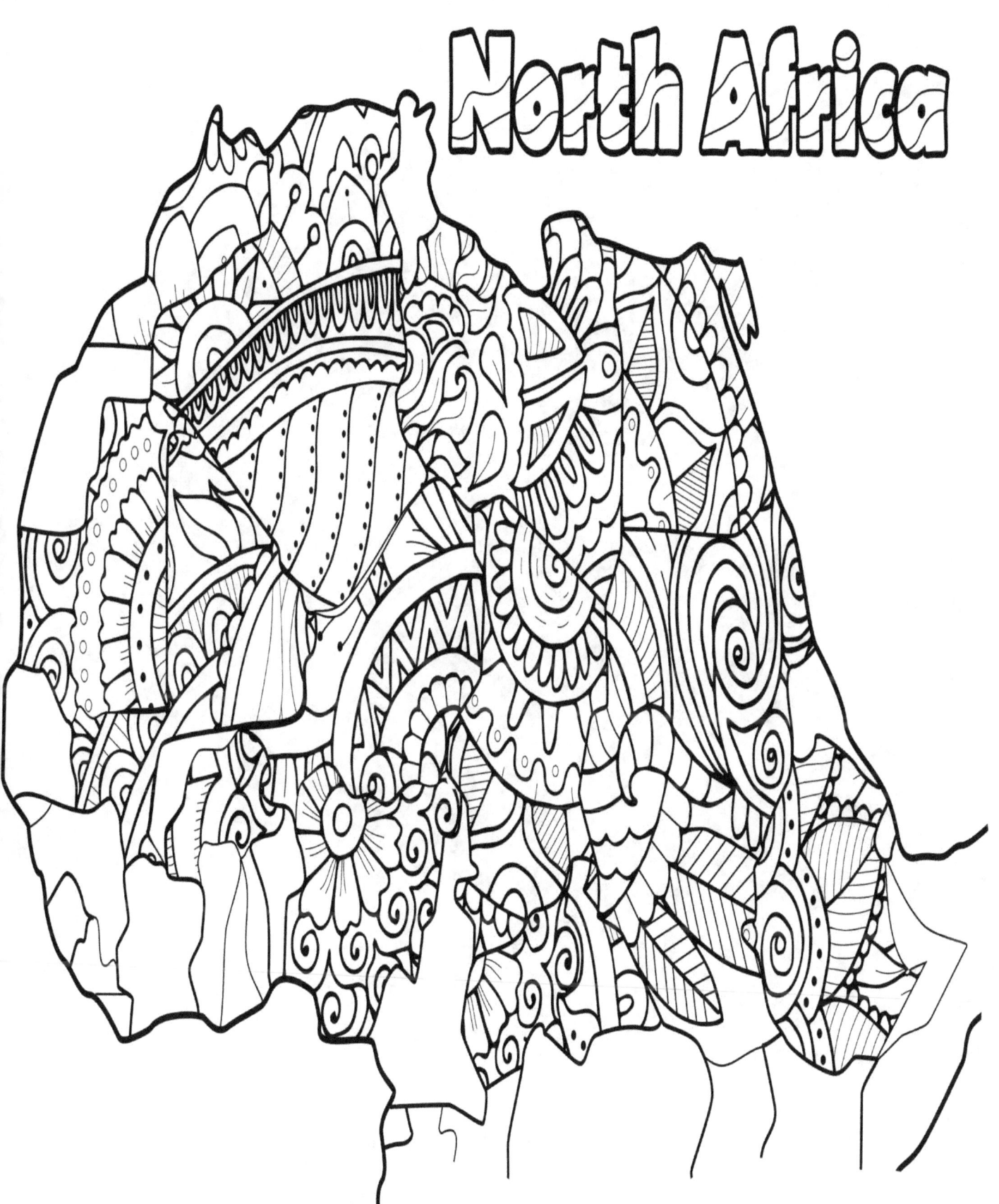

North Africa

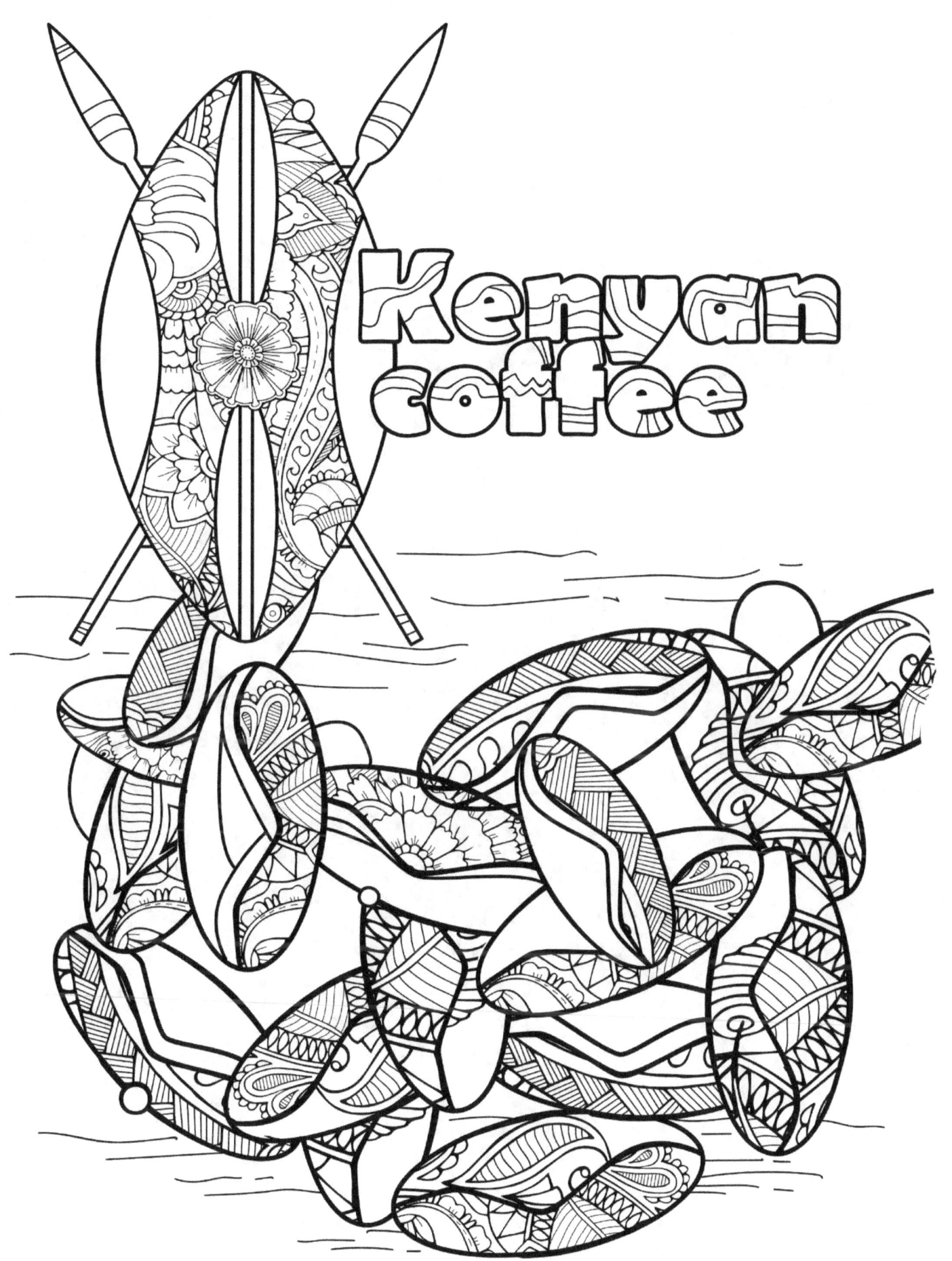

Other Coloring Books from Aryla Publishing

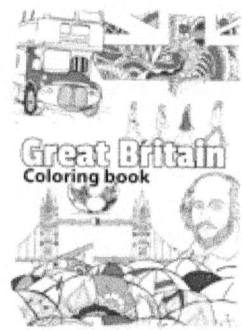 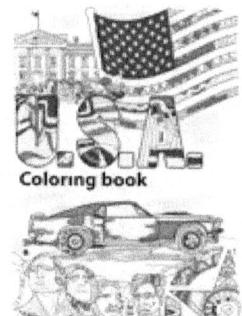 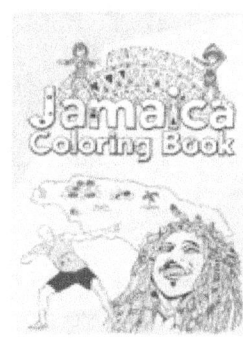 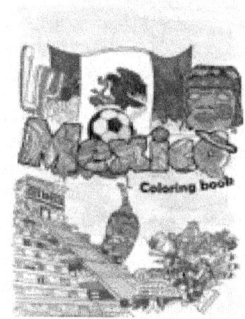 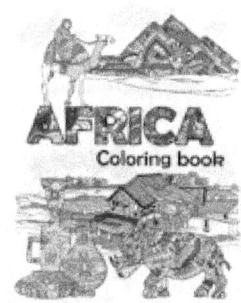

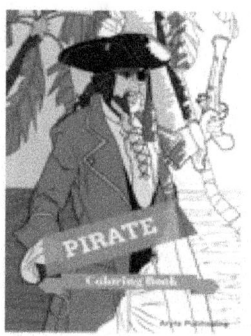 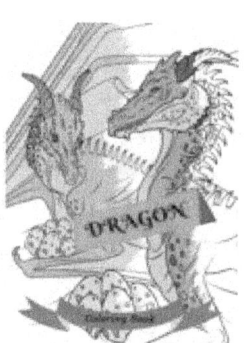 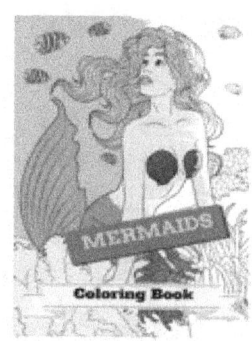 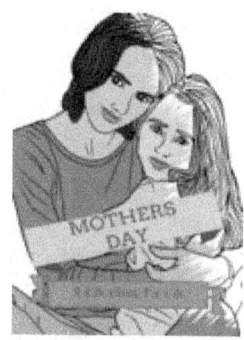 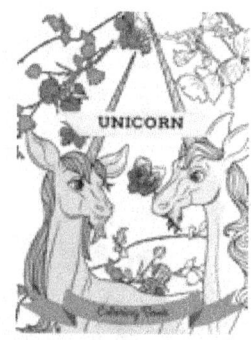

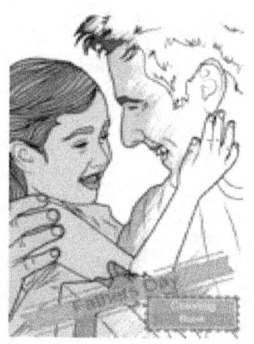 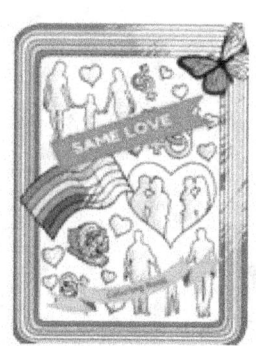 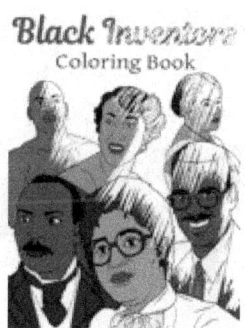 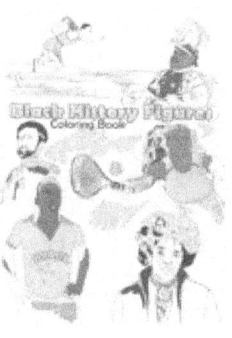

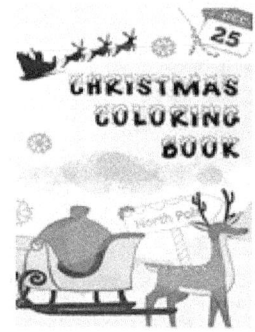 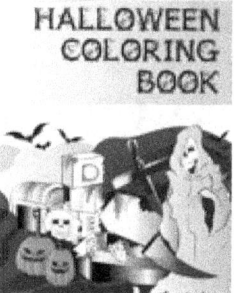 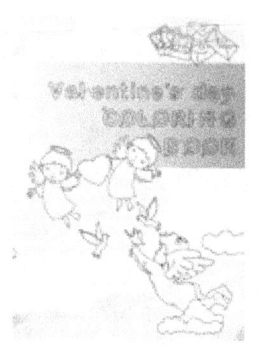 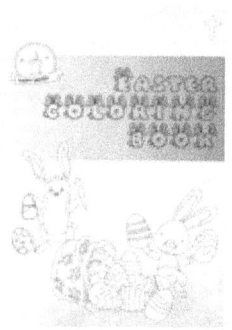

www.ingramcontent.com/pod-product-compliance
Lightning Source LLC
Chambersburg PA
CBHW081742220526
45468CB00008B/2208

* 9 7 8 1 9 1 2 6 7 5 2 4 1 *